SHADOW EMPEROR

Shawn Boonstra

with Clifford Goldstein

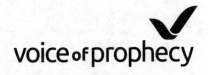

voice of prophecy

and Pacific Press Publishing Association

Cover Illustration & Design by Palmer Halvorson
Interior Design by Mark Bond
Text Typeset: Bembo 10/13

Copyright © 2016 by the Voice of Prophecy. All Rights Reserved.

Additional copies of this book, a DVD version of the series,
and many other spiritual resources are available by calling
toll-free 1-877-877-2487 or by visiting **vop.com/store**.

Unless otherwise marked, all Scripture verses are
quoted from NKJV, the New King James Version®.
Copyright © 1982 by Thomas Nelson, Inc.
Used by permission. All rights reserved.

Scripture quotations marked NASB are taken from the
New American Standard Bible®, Copyright © 1960, 1962, 1963, 1968,
1971, 1972, 1973, 1975, 1977, 1995 by The Lockman Foundation.
Used by permission. (www.Lockman.org)

Scripture quotations marked KJV are from
the King James Version of the Bible.

Printed in the United States of America by
Pacific Press Publishing Association, Nampa, Idaho.
www.pacificpress.com

ISBN: 978-0-8163-6128-1

CONTENTS

FOREWORD

There have been hundreds, if not thousands, of volumes written on the life of the Roman Emperor Constantine. Yet even with all that coverage, it remains difficult to estimate the impact this one illustrious man has had on Western civilization. While the average citizen is not generally conversant in the history of his life, his name is still recognizable to almost everyone. He has made regular appearances in historical books, television documentaries, and Hollywood productions. He has been accused of much, credited with much, and claimed by many, whether in an attempt to own or strategically *dis*own him.

It is not the purpose of this little book to provide an exhaustive account of his life, or even a searching analysis of his contribution to the long and complex history of Christianity. This short volume was written as a companion to the Voice of Prophecy documentary series *Shadow Empire*, and provides a thumbnail sketch—a review, really—of the content covered in that production.

It is a starting point, designed to raise as many questions as it answers, and intended to start the reader on the path to discovery.

Shawn Boonstra
March 2016

CHAPTER ONE

Niš is a small city in the heart of Serbia. It is a pleasant place today—a bustling town with a lot of different industries and businesses. It is the third largest city in Serbia, behind Belgrade and Novi Sad, with about 180,000 residents.

The cost of living is attractive, and so are the surroundings. The city straddles the Nišava River, and is ringed by gorgeous mountains. You couldn't ask for a nicer place to live. If not for the fact that the Balkan region was ground zero for World War I, and has been the site of many conflicts since, it would be tempting to think of it as a near-perfect place to live.

Niš is a very modern city, with an upscale shopping district and most of the urban conveniences you'd expect in Europe. But the city is very old—one of the oldest in all of Europe. The Celts had settled the region in the 3rd century BC; the Romans conquered it in 75 BC and named it Naissus. Situated in the land that separated Europe from Asia Minor, it was considered an important gateway between the eastern and western parts of the empire. The Romans built a vast military highway in the 1st century, known as the Via Militaris, with Naissus becoming one of the key towns along the long route.

The city is not only old, but it plays a pivotal role in the history of Rome; in fact, it played a much bigger role than anyone could have ever anticipated. About 1,700 years ago, a baby was born under a cloud of illegitimacy to a humble and insignificant village girl. That might not seem like a big deal to those of us living in the 21st century, because babies are born to unwed, unknown girls with some frequency. It happens every day.

But in this case, however, it was a baby who would grow up to completely transform the whole world. Even today, most of us still live in his shadow. It's not likely anybody pointed it out in your history classes, but he has impacted the way you live, think, and believe. We live in his shadow. His fingerprints are all over western culture, even after the passage of many centuries. With the exception of Jesus of Nazareth, and perhaps Saul of Tarsus, no other person in Christian history has shaped the world to the extent of this one man.

Who is he?

Constantine.

When he *did* come up in history class, you were probably introduced to him as Constantine the Great. What you are about to read is a quick thumbnail sketch of his incredible and powerfully influential life.

In the year AD 271, a tired Roman military tribune, Flavius Constantius, led his men back from a key battle with the Sarmatians, a large confederation of ancient Persians who had been slowly making their way westward for centuries. Eventually, with the help of Germanic barbarians (notably the Goths), they started pushing their way deep into Roman territory, something the empire could not allow. The barbarian tribes had been making life hard for Roman citizens, especially those who lived in the outer regions of the empire. Barbarian raids had been disrupting Roman peace for many years.

Flavius Constantius defeated the Sarmatians decisively, and on his way back from the front, he traveled the road that brought him through Naissus. It was an ideal place to rest.

We're not exactly sure how long they had been away from home, but Roman soldiers were away often and worked hard, so it's not difficult to imagine that after a hard-won battle, they were ready for a break, even if it was just a single good night's sleep. It appears that Flavius Constantius himself needed a break—and a distraction.

Military life being what it was, the rank-and-file soldiers spent the night in the fields adjacent to the village, left to fight the elements and mosquitoes. Constantius, as commander, fared considerably better than his men by securing lodging in the village inn, a place where he could get a good meal, a great night's sleep—and unfortunately, something else that soldiers sometimes go looking for in a port of call: a little company for the evening.

According to the ancient story, recorded for us by a Greek monk, Flavius Constantius asked the local innkeeper to find him a female companion for the night—a practice seemingly as old as the profession itself. While distasteful, such behavior wasn't uncommon.

The usual practice in Naissus was to find a widow to serve the needs of a "worthy" sojourner, but that night, the innkeeper dispensed with the usual, because he was deeply impressed by the stature and regal bearing of this clearly important Roman. At 23 years of age, Flavius was "tall, slender, of fair complexion and grey-blue eyes, and an elegant nose." He cut a striking figure. For this reason—and perhaps to get on the good side of a clearly important man—the innkeeper did the unthinkable. He sent for his 16-year-old virgin daughter, and ordered her to go in and spend the night with the Roman.

If it happened today, it would be a crime, but 1,700 years ago, it wasn't unheard of. Modern students of history must resist the temptation to read 21st century morals and more into the story of yesterday. Lives were shorter and adult expectations kicked in sooner. Christians in particular should remember that Bible scholars estimate that Mary, the mother of Jesus, was likely about that same age when she gave birth to Jesus—although her circumstances were obviously different.

What happened was nearly normal. What *wasn't* normal, however, was a father giving up his own daughter for the night; wars have been fought over slighter indiscretions. Nevertheless, tied hopelessly to a lifetime of hardship and poverty, the innkeeper may have believed that surrendering his daughter might one day lead to something good for his family (if he only knew!), so he gave his daughter to the Roman commander.

Her name was Helena, and if that name seems familiar, it's because of what happened that night. Her rendezvous with the soldier meant she would become one of the most famous women in history.

In the words of an imaginative monk who recounted the story, Constantius, falling asleep after having the girl, saw in his sleep "the sun rise against nature from the ocean in the West and come to bathe in brilliance the house where Constantius and Helena were asleep. Constantius was awed by the vision, being superstitious, i.e., a fervent believer in his religion, and thought that it was Apollo who was seeing his actions from above. Terrified and speechless, he drew away from the erotic embraces, fearful that he might have offended the gods."[1]

How the monk actually knew what happened that night is a bit of a mystery, but the fact that he recounted it so vividly does suggest that, even in his day, the idea of an older man deflowering a 16-year-old girl merely for his own pleasure wasn't considered moral. Flavius felt guilty, proving the words of the Apostle Paul in his letter to the Romans. Writing about pagans who didn't know the religion of Jesus, Paul wrote:

> *For when Gentiles, who do not have the law, by nature do the things in the law, these, although not having the law, are a law to themselves, who show the work of the law written in their hearts, their conscience also bearing witness, and between themselves their thoughts accusing or else excusing them. (Romans 2:14, 15)*

Flavius' thoughts were accusing him. The next morning, when the sun came through the bedroom window, he suddenly became worried that what he had done to the young girl had offended the sun god, Apollo. He wasted no time leaving town. Just before he left, however, he gave a sum of money to the innkeeper, and then he handed the man something else—an item that would later signal a turning point in history. He gave the man his purple tribunal cape—a fairly significant gift to leave with a common peasant. It had a buckle with his initials and his military rank.

"Keep the maiden pure," he said (ironic!), "and if by chance she gives birth to a child, protect that child as the apple of your eye."[2]

Then he turned and left, probably thinking that he would never return, and likely certain he would never see the young woman again. Considering the usual nature of wanton traveling men, perhaps he didn't want to. He was keen to return to life as usual.

Helena, of course, didn't have that option, because she was now pregnant. Her father's thoughtless gesture changed the course of her life—and the world.

She gave birth to a boy, whom she named Constantine, after his father: "Little Constantius." The father, of course, had no idea that he existed. What stories his mother and grandfather told him growing up, we do not know. We have no idea if he was aware of his true identity.

Given Constantine's close ties to Christianity, some might compare his situation to that of the boy Jesus. While not precisely the same, there *are* some interesting comparisons. Jesus was also born under a cloud of illegitimacy: His mother had no husband when she became pregnant, leading her fiancé Joseph to suspect adultery.

We are told very little about Jesus' childhood years, and the biblical record isn't entirely clear about when He became fully aware of His true parentage. Constantine would have to prove that his father was important; Jesus would have to prove that His Father was the God of Israel.

While the peasant boy was growing up in Naissus, his father's life was taking a turn for the best. While his legions were in Pannonia, near the banks of the mighty Danube River, Constantius was suddenly summoned to the tent of the emperor, Carus. Carus, though previously a Roman general, had been named emperor after Emperor Probus was murdered about eight months earlier, in AD 282, by soldiers who, it seems, didn't like his orders to perform civil tasks, such as draining marshes. At the tent, Carus told Flavius Constantius, now 33 years old, that he wanted him to become the governor of Dalmatia, a region now located in modern-day Croatia.

The appointment was a big deal, because Dalmatia was a key Roman territory, where the empire controlled the flow of trade between east and west. If you became the governor of *that* region, it meant you were going places.

And Constantius was a man determined to go places.

Though this appointment was, indeed, a big career boost for Flavius Constantius, it also sealed the fate of Helena and little Constantine. Rome was a highly stratified society, and things like status, name, and family were very important. It wasn't like America, where hard work, good luck, and good business sense can catapult you to the top. In Rome, generally, the social stratum you were born to was, generally, the social stratum you died in.

The divide between Helena and Flavius Constantius couldn't have gotten much wider: one was a humble peasant woman, a nobody in the world of the Romans, and the other was now perched at the top of Roman society, governor of a crucially important region.

Though without newspapers, the Roman Empire wasn't devoid of news. Constantius was now famous and influential enough that Helena probably knew exactly where he was. Attempting to contact him, however, would have been futile. The Roman world was not egalitarian, and a village girl would have had no way to communicate with the father. It wouldn't have been allowed.

It should have been the end of the story. Helena and Constantine may well have been non-existent: just another baby born to another peasant girl, two unimportant people swallowed up by the vast masses of humanity, the millions and even billions who have lived and died on earth—long gone, long forgotten, buried by history.

Except that, almost a decade later, something remarkable happened. Or, as the writer D. G. Kousoulas expressed it in his landmark biography of Constantine: "This might have been the end of the story and we would have never heard of a peasant boy in Naissus named Constantine had fate not intervened."[3]

What happened a decade later? Another group of horsemen, Roman troops, stopped at the village inn in Naissus to spend the evening. In the morning, when they came out to the barn, they found little Constantine, now nine years old, teasing their horses. They were infuriated by the audacity of the peasant child, so they started beating him.

His mother, now in her mid-twenties, heard the commotion and came running into the barn. "Don't you know who that is?" she yelled. "You are beating the governor's son!"

They looked her over and started laughing. How in the world could *this* woman's son belong to the Roman governor? She didn't *look* like the kind of woman he'd be interested in: rough-hewn peasant garb, messy hair, dirty hands and face from working in the kitchen and garden.

"Do you take us for fools?" they answered.

They probably had a few other choice words as well.

"I swear to the gods that I am telling you the truth," she explained. "When Flavius Constantius was a tribune, he slept here on his way back from the war with the Sarmatians, and I became pregnant and gave birth to this boy. And if you want to know the truth, I can give you evidence—my reward for going to bed with him."[4]

They must have wondered: *What evidence could there be?* She ran back into the house, and came back with something in her arms: a cape. A *tribunal* cape. One can only imagine the panic those men must have felt when they saw the initials on the buckle: Flavius Constantius, who was, indeed, the governor of Dalmatia.

Though more details are lost to history, the jesting and mocking likely stopped instantly. Romans took things like lineage very seriously. They took their military superiors even more seriously.

Instead of covering their tracks, these rough soldiers did the right thing: they went to inform the governor that he had a son living in the village of Naissus. Even joking with him, they told him the boy looked just like him. "The child," they said, "is your spit and image, Domine."

The news got even better. Instead of just brushing off the report, as he could have easily done, the governor was apparently delighted. Though this could have caused big problems for him, a headache he didn't need, his paternal instincts kicked in and he sent for the woman and the child.

Helena was now 26 years old, and the reunion went as well as one could imagine. She was welcomed into the governor's house with open arms.

The move from Naissus must have provided plenty of culture shock for Helena and her son. They only knew the coarse and hard world of a small town in Dalmatia. What did they know of palaces, of marble columns, of luxurious baths? How could they hope to relate to the highest circles of Roman society?

According to the surviving historical accounts, Flavius Constantius was thrilled to have them in his home, especially the boy. He was, after all, his son—even named after him. The jesting soldiers were right: the boy did, indeed, resemble him. As a high-ranking official, he was well within his rights to send them away, but he didn't. Helena and Constantine were home to stay.

Helena was now 10 years older, and surely the life of a peasant had left its marks. But, still, she was only 26-years old, and it seems that Constantius found her attractive enough to consider marrying her.

There was a problem: an actual marriage was, really, out of the question. There was no way Flavius Constantius could marry a mere peasant—and not because he thought he was too good for her. In fact, he also originated from a humble peasant village. He had been raised by shepherds just a few miles north of where he now lived.

The problem was that Roman custom and tradition just didn't allow for it. The social divide was too great. She could live in his house, but she couldn't be his wife, at least in the full sense of the term.

He settled on another solution. He could have simply kept her, kind of like a concubine, but that would have made his son what was called a *nothos*, an illegitimate child who would have lacked his father's name. If Constantine didn't have his father's name, he would not have been considered an actual member of his family, and could not claim the advantages of civil law. Not wanting such a stain on his child, the father took advantage of a lesser form of marriage: *matrimonium concubinatum*, a form of matrimony that Roman law allowed in certain cases. Helena was legally tied to him, and the "marriage" gave the child certain legal rights when it came to inheritance and the like. What mattered most, though, at least for Constantius, was that his son was now deemed legitimate.

Again, one can only imagine what a culture shock both the mother and son faced: one day impoverished backwater peasants, the next living in the luxury of a Roman governor's mansion. (It was probably the first time in their lives the two ever saw the sea, because the mansion itself rested along the coast.)

But the change cut both ways, too. Flavius Constantius suddenly had uneducated peasants living with him, and they were now family. They were going to have to learn how to live in this new environment. They were illiterate, and they could speak only Dardanian, with a few Latin and Greek words thrown in for good measure. Constantius quickly set out the task of teaching them both to read and write. Tutors began the work, and one can imagine the child learning more quickly than the mother, but it seems, over time, they progressed, especially the boy.

In the words of Constantine biographer, Kousoulas: "The little peasant boy was changing rapidly, his quick curious mind taking in every snippet of knowledge, every new experience, doing exceedingly well in his schooling and in the athletic exercises that were part of his daily routine. Constantius was proud of his son and could look to the future with confidence, but neither he nor Helena could have the slightest notion that someday the precocious boy would become the new emperor who would destroy the ancient idols and usher in the era of a new faith."[5]

But now we're jumping ahead, to a future not yet realized. For now, to understand all the threads in this story, we need to go back, to the even deeper past, in order to better grasp the background that helped pave the way for this small child to one day assume the role of emperor and get the name Constantine the Great.

FOOTNOTES FOR CHAPTER ONE

1.   Kousoulas, D. George. *The Life and Times of Constantine the Great*. Bethesda, MD: Rutledge, 2007. Print, 7.

2.   Ibid.

3.   Ibid., 8.

4.   Ibid., 9.

5.   Ibid., 12.

CHAPTER TWO

THERE IS A BRIDGE IN ROME, NOT FAR FROM the Vatican, known locally as Ponte Fabricio. It's a popular spot for tourists and artists, connecting two parts of the city and passing over an island in the middle of the Tiber River.

It is likely the oldest structure in the neighborhood, having been built some 60 years before the birth of Christ. Quite unlike other structures that old, however, which lie in various states of ruin, the bridge is still in use. In fact, it has been in *continuous* use since it was first built.

It's a remarkable example of Roman engineering skill. The Romans were builders. They managed to build an international infrastructure of roads, highways, bridges, and aqueducts that helped weld together an empire made up of hundreds of different cultures and nationalities. There were the Jews to the east, the barbarians to the north, and the ancient civilizations of Greece, Persia, and North Africa—all in one empire that was, in spite of its wide variety, remarkably stable and peaceful.

After Augustus Caesar's famous victory at the Battle of Actium in 27 BC, the Roman Empire suddenly became very secure and predictable. It was, in spite of the occasional brutality of Roman troops, a good place to live, especially when compared to places outside the empire that were constantly under the threat of one invader or another.

It was *Pax Romana*—the peace of Rome. From Northern Europe to North Africa, from Spain to the Middle East, citizens and subjects could count on Roman water, Roman highways, Roman courts, and Roman law (both the good and the bad). The Romans brought structure to daily life. Even though the people were mostly conquered subjects, most of them actually *liked* living in the world of the Roman Empire. *Pax Romana* lasted for roughly 200 years—from 27 BC to AD 180—and it gave rise to unprecedented peace and economic prosperity throughout the empire. During this time, the Roman Empire also reached its peak in terms of land area, and its population swelled to an estimated 70 million people.

One theory as to why this worked so well was the fact that Rome had a larger-than-life person at the head: the emperor. He was the ideological glue that held the empire together: a focal point for unity. Conquered subjects had almost absolute freedom of conscience. Under Rome, they could worship whatever god and observe whatever religious rituals they wanted. In contrast to other societies of the time, Rome was remarkably tolerant.

There was just one caveat. The people of the conquered realms could continue with the religion of their ancestors, but they also had to acknowledge the deity of the Roman emperor. He was considered the embodiment of Roma, the goddess of Rome, and needed to be respected as such. To reject the emperor's divinity was to question the validity of the empire itself.

Now, in reality, most people didn't really think that the emperor was a divine being, especially if you happened to grow up with the man or go to school with him. Shakespeare highlights this fact in his play, *Julius Caesar*, in which he created a

scene where a fellow Roman, Cassius, recounts the occasion
when he had to rescue the young Caesar from drowning in the
Tiber River:

> *I was born free as Caesar; so were you:*
> *We both have fed as well, and we can both*
> *Endure the winter's cold as well as he:*
> *For once, upon a raw and gusty day,*
> *The troubled Tiber chafing with her shores,*
> *Caesar said to me "Darest thou, Cassius, now*
> *Leap in with me into this angry flood,*
> *And swim to yonder point?" Upon the word,*
> *Accoutred as I was, I plunged in*
> *And bade him follow; so indeed he did.*
> *The torrent roar'd, and we did buffet it*
> *With lusty sinews, throwing it aside*
> *And stemming it with hearts of controversy;*
> *But ere we could arrive the point proposed,*
> *Caesar cried "Help me, Cassius, or I sink!"*
> *I, as Aeneas, our great ancestor,*
> *Did from the flames of Troy upon his shoulder*
> *The old Anchises bear, so from the waves of Tiber*
> *Did I the tired Caesar. And this man*
> *Is now become a god, and Cassius is*
> *A wretched creature and must bend his body.*[6]

The people who surrounded the emperor knew that he
wasn't a god. People were well familiar with the humanity
of their ruler, but that was not the point. During the reign of
Augustus Caesar, the unity and hard-won peace of the empire

became so important that emperor worship just became a tangible way to reinforce national unity. You knew that he wasn't really a god, but you offered him a little worship in order to prove your allegiance to the gods of Rome. It was a mere ceremonial act—a veneration that pointed to something bigger.

In later years, all you really had to do in order to demonstrate your solidarity with Rome was offer a pinch of incense to the emperor, just once in a while, and then you could go back to life as normal. You were free to worship the god or goddess you really believed in.

There was a notable exception to the requirement: the Jews. They had special privileges and a national exemption, granted to them by Julius Caesar because they had proven helpful during his conquests. They didn't have to acknowledge the emperor as a god; they only had to promise to pray for him and for the health of the empire.

The Jews were only too happy to do it, and there was a biblical parallel for the practice. Many centuries earlier, when the Jews were in Babylonian captivity, the Lord told them through the prophet Jeremiah to do much the same thing: "And seek the peace of the city where I have caused you to be carried away captive, and pray to the Lord for it; for in its peace you will have peace." (Jeremiah 29:7)

Praying for the emperor wasn't a problem, but worshipping him was.

The Romans had a word for the Jewish faith. They called it *religio*. If that looks familiar, it's because *religio* is the root of our word "religion." To the Romans, a *religio* was a national faith, one that defined an entire nation. They were familiar with national religions; Rome was built on the concept.

But what of the Christians? Were they also considered a *religio?*

In their earliest days, the answer seems to have been yes. As far as the average Roman could tell, there was really no difference between Jews and Christians. The Jews already had a number of factions within their religion—Pharisees, Sadducees, Essenes, etc.—and the Christians appeared to be just one more division. Their Teacher, Jesus of Nazareth, was a practicing Jew. His followers addressed Him as "Rabbi." The first disciples were all Jews, and the Scripture of the Christian church, which in the very first years consisted of only the Old Testament, was a Jewish document. As the New Testament came into being, it was also written by Jews—with the possible exception of Luke's contributions.

By all appearances, Christians were Jews. For the first few centuries, they even continued to observe the seventh-day Sabbath.

As time progressed, however, a radical separation took place between the two groups, especially after the destruction of the Jerusalem Temple in AD 70. Though many details are lost, it is widely believed that as more and more Gentiles joined the faith, more and more Jewish practices began to disappear. History suggests that some synagogues began to include a curse on "Nazarenes"—the followers of Jesus—in order to root out the Christians in their midst, who would be exposed by their refusal to participate in the prayer:

> *For the apostates let there be no hope. And let the arrogant government be speedily uprooted in our days. Let the nozerim and the minim be destroyed in a moment. And let them be blotted out of the Book of Life and not be inscribed together with the righteous. Blessed art thou, O Lord, who humblest the arrogant.*[7]

The *nozerim* were the Christians. As the divide grew sharper over the years, it also became harder for those of the Jewish faith to become followers of Jesus, and while the Jews of Israel and western Christians mostly consider themselves political allies in the Middle East, the religious divide between Jew and Christian continues to be deep.

As the rift became more obvious, the Romans began to look at Christians in a new light. They were no longer considered a *religio*, a national religion. Instead, they were considered a *superstitio,* which gave rise to our word "superstition." A *superstitio* was a mere sect, a set of religious beliefs that did *not* provide national identity. The difference between a *religio* and a *superstitio* was not unlike our modern distinction between "mainstream religion" and a "cult" or "sect." A *superstitio* simply did not have the widespread acceptance or respectability of a *religio*.

As the distinction between Christian and Jew became more obvious, the Christians were no longer sheltered by the Jewish exemption, and that meant that they, too, would be required to pay obeisance to the emperor, an act that was just as problematic for them as it was for their Jewish cousins.

The middle of the 3rd century provides a great example of the problem faced by early Christians. There were likely about 30,000 Christians living in the city of Rome at the time, and the emperor Trajan Decius (Roman emperor from AD 249 to 251) passed a law saying that every male citizen was required to buy a sacrificial animal, bring it to the temple for ritual cooking, publicly consume some of the meat, and then offer some wine to the "genius"—or the guiding spirit of the emperor.

It was an act of worship, clearly recognizing the divinity of the emperor, and a mandatory act of allegiance to the empire.

Those who performed the ritual received proof: a signed certificate. Those who didn't were considered traitors—and as most people know, the Romans didn't take kindly to traitors.

One scholar expressed it like this:"All the inhabitants of the empire were required to sacrifice before the magistrates of their community 'for the safety of the empire' by a certain day (the date would vary from place to place and the order may have been that the sacrifice had to be completed within a specified period after a community received the edict). When they sacrificed they would obtain a certificate (libellus) recording the fact that they had complied with the order. That is, the certificate would testify the sacrificant's loyalty to the ancestral gods and to the consumption of sacrificial food and drink as well as the names of the officials who were overseeing the sacrifice."[8]

At other times, under other emperors, the ritual was less elaborate. All you really had to do was offer a pinch of incense—a token ritual proving your loyalty. For the most part, Christians didn't have a problem with a degree of loyalty to an earthly king, because their Scriptures taught them to be good citizens. In fact, in one place, Peter instructed his readers: "Honor the king." (1 Peter 2:17) It was a startling statement for Peter to make, because the king they were likely being asked to honor was, of all people, the Emperor Nero.

For almost every other subjugated people, the requirement was no big deal. But Christians were monotheists, just like their Jewish predecessors. They acknowledged the existence of only one God—and that God, they said, had come to Earth in human form. He had been put to death on a Roman cross, and then He rose from the dead. That part of the faith seemed silly to most Romans—at best, if the story was true, Jesus had merely outsmarted a few Roman officials. But the doctrine of the Second Coming was far more problematic: Jesus was coming back to judge the living and the dead—and then He would sweep aside all earthly empires and establish a Kingdom of His own.

The book of Daniel predicted the rise and fall of many great empires (Babylon, Medo-Persia, Greece, and even Rome). Even though Daniel clearly predicted that Rome would attain to great heights and power (and actually exist in one form or another until the end of the world), Roman hegemony would not last forever. The Kingdom of Christ, the Stone who crushes the statue of worldly government (see Daniel 2), the One whom the Christians worshipped, would ultimately prevail. Here's how the prophet Daniel described it in his stunning depiction of heaven's judgment: "Then to Him was given dominion and glory and a kingdom, that all peoples, nations, and languages should serve Him. His dominion is an everlasting dominion, which shall not pass away, and His kingdom the one which shall not be destroyed." (Daniel 7:14)

The Christians would have also had an issue with offering a sacrifice, another distinction between the burgeoning church and its Jewish antecedent. In Christian theology, all sacrifices, in their original meaning, were *types,* or symbols, which meant that they pointed forward to *antitypes,* or fulfillments. The sacrificial animals in the Jerusalem Temple were object lessons in the Gospel, pointing forward to the Lamb of God who would come to take away the sin of the world. (John 1:29) The altar of sacrifice, located in the courtyard of the temple, pointed forward to the atoning death of Christ on the cross. As the author of the book of Hebrews wrote: "But this Man, after He had offered one sacrifice for sins forever, sat down at the right hand of God." (Hebrews 10:12)

Christians were, by and large, good Roman citizens, but emperor worship was out of the question. Their worship was reserved for Christ alone.

The Christians were therefore perceived as a clear threat to *Pax Romana*. They were an unstable element in the empire, and the Romans could never be sure that they would be loyal subjects, because they clearly reserved their highest allegiance for a different King. Caesar would never be their priority, and neither would Rome.

Roman distrust of Christianity grew, and the fact that most Christians distanced themselves from key aspects of Roman culture didn't help, either. Christians weren't keen on Roman entertainment, for example, because it was graphically violent, and Christians worshipped a "Prince of Peace." (Isaiah 9:6) Romans pitted gladiators against each other in fights to the death in order to provide public entertainment. There is some indication that occasionally, when a Roman play called for a death scene, condemned prisoners were actually murdered on stage to make the drama seem more realistic. Christians could not reconcile the teachings of Jesus with entertainment that appealed to such base instincts. They worshipped a Creator rather than a destroyer. Jesus was a God of love and redemption.

The Christians were seldom seen in the entertainment hotspots of the day, which reinforced the idea that they were distinctly *not* Roman.

There was also the issue of health care: a lot of the hospitals were dedicated to the pagan gods of healing, which in itself wasn't a big problem, because few people care about the religious beliefs of the doctor who sets a broken bone. But in some places, the priest of the serpent god Asclepius would perform his rituals over you. (Asclepius is usually depicted with a serpent wrapped around a staff, a variation on the Rod of Hermes, which can still be seen in some medical establishments to this day. The mere presence of a Roman symbol is obviously not an issue for modern Christians, but if they were required to participate in rituals that violate the teachings of Jesus, most Christians would likely abstain today.) Christians were not able to participate in such rituals in good conscience.

Public education also posed a bit of a problem, because the value system taught by Roman educators was essentially at odds with Christian beliefs. In the earliest years of Christianity, this wasn't typically a big problem, since most Christians belonged to the lower, uneducated classes, but as time moved along, it became more of an issue. If you sent your kids to a Roman teacher, they would be subjected to pagan religion. They would learn different theories about philosophical truth, the origin of the human race, and the meaning of life. And while Christians have never shied away from other peoples' ideas, they didn't really want to expose their children to contrary ideas at such a young and impressionable age.

Christians living in the Roman Empire were, by and large, countercultural. But more issues arose as well.

In the 2nd century, another emperor sent a new governor to Asia Minor to rule a region called Bithynia. There was one town in that region where people were complaining bitterly about Christians. The issue seems odd at first glance: *the local butchers weren't selling enough meat.*

How were the Christians at fault? It's not hard to guess. A lot of the meat being sold was earmarked for sacrifices to the pagan gods. However, the influence of the Christians had put a massive dent in meat sales. People who listened to their preaching often quit offering sacrifices. Believers in Jesus knew that the need for sacrifices was over. The true and only *needed* Sacrifice had been offered once and for all: Jesus on the cross.

And of course, any act of obeisance to the Roman gods was strictly off-limits.

When meat sales plummeted, the butchers blamed the Christians for their economic woes—and probably with good reason.

At first, the new governor of Bythinia, Pliny the Younger, didn't see a problem. He wrote to the emperor, who had heard the complaints, and said, "I really don't know what all the fuss is about—I still see all kinds of meat for sale in the market. I think the butchers are exaggerating the problem."

Facts seldom matter in a world where people want a scapegoat, especially when those problems involve putting bread on the table. So even though the accusation against the Christians had little substance, Pliny executed a few Christians to appease the masses, reasoning that killing a few people to keep the rest of the community happy was probably worthwhile.

Truth be told, Pliny was reasonably happy to see a few Christians die, because he personally found them distasteful. He found them completely inflexible in their beliefs and actions, unwilling to compromise—and everybody knows that good politics always involves compromise.

Hatred of Christians was growing. Across the Roman Empire, anti-Christian pamphlets started to circulate. Wherever the average Roman citizen was struggling to understand the beliefs and lifestyles of their Christian neighbors, the rumor mill began to fill in the blanks.

It was said that Christians met in secret, which in many places was absolutely true. Christians *had* to meet in secret because Romans were deeply suspicious of any meeting that involved more than a handful of people; it smacked of insurrection. If a group grew to more than a dozen people, it might become a breeding ground for political unrest and become, in effect, the equivalent of a modern terrorist cell. There was enough precedent across the empire's history to make Romans nervous.

Then word spread that when the Christians met in secret, they participated in cannibalism: eating human flesh and drinking human blood. Of course, what they were hearing about was the Christian communion service, a symbolic ritual designed to remind believers of the sacrificial death of Jesus at the cross, a ceremonial meal (and descendant of Passover) instituted by Jesus Himself:

> For I received from the Lord that which I also delivered to you: that the Lord Jesus on the same night in which He was betrayed took bread; and when He had given thanks, He broke it and said, "Take, eat; this is My body which is broken for you; do this in remembrance of Me." In the same manner He also took the cup after supper, saying, "This cup is the new covenant in My blood. This do, as often as you drink it, in remembrance of Me." For as often as you eat this bread and drink this cup, you proclaim the Lord's death till He comes. (1 Corinthians 11:23-26)

There was no actual consumption of flesh or blood, but facts seldom matter in a world where political mistrust demands a scapegoat narrative. There was no cannibalism, but because many Christians met away from prying eyes, the rumors seemed likely, and conveniently fed a desire to remove Christians from the community.

There was also talk of incest. The communion service was sometimes referred to as a "love feast," which to the Roman mind was comparable to an orgy. In fact, the Christians were speaking of *agape* love, which is a sacrificial, self-denying love. It was the kind of love Jesus described: "Greater love (*agape*) has no one than this, than to lay down one's life for his friends." (John 15:13)

The "agape feast" was a celebration of Jesus' selfless love for the sinful human race—a love that led Him to give His life in order to save us.

Agape stands in contrast to another Greek word for love, *eros. Eros* is the root of our word *erotic,* and meant pretty much the same thing. *Eros* love is based on desire, and it answers to lust and self-gratification. The Romans indulged *eros* in their orgies; the Christians celebrated *agape* at the communion service.

The concept of a God who loved the human race enough to sacrifice self was foreign to Roman mythology, which was suffused with self-serving, arbitrary, and capricious gods who toyed with the human race for their own amusement. The only "love" known to such gods was *eros,* and some Romans duly celebrated those gods with drunken and wanton orgies. When they heard that the Christians had "love feasts," they attributed the same behavior to them—with a difference. The Christians also referred to each other as "brother" and "sister," so the rumor spread that they were indulging in orgies with family members.

Between the accusations of cannibalism and incestuous orgies, the Christians became pariahs. It was at this moment in history when all those stories about Christians being thrown to the lions started to unfold.

We don't know of any Christians who actually died in the Colosseum itself, but they were put to death in many other venues in Rome. At one point, Nero apparently had Christians dipped in tar, nailed to crosses, and then lit on fire so that he could use them as night lights at his games. They were wrapped in animal skins and fed to wild animals. They became the outcasts of Roman society, and they were deemed to be the cause of many problems. From the French Revolution to the Holocaust, despotic powers have always needed scapegoats—people who could shoulder the blame when something went wrong, and in the first few centuries of the church's existence, the Christians were a lightning rod for Rome's wrath.

Toward the end of the first century, large sections of the city of Rome suddenly burned to the ground. People like to say that Nero fiddled while Rome burned, but the truth is that he was likely out of town when the fire broke out. Still, the rumor mill began to suggest that Nero may have started the fire himself in order to make room for his own grandiose building projects. Politically, he couldn't afford to wear the blame, and so he needed a scapegoat.

The Christians were a convenient target. A new rumor spread throughout the city: "We've heard that Christians say that the world will end in fire, and we think they started *this* fire to make their own prophecy come true."

Of course, it was another distortion of what Christians *really* believed. It was true that they taught the world would end in fire, but that fire would not—could not—be started by human hands: "But the day of the Lord will come as a thief in the night, in which the heavens will pass away with a great noise, and the elements will melt with fervent heat; both the earth and the works that are in it will be burned up." (2 Peter 3:10)

The prediction of Daniel that God would eventually obliterate human kingdoms and establish one of His own compared the coming Kingdom—to be realized at the Second Coming of Christ—to a stone smashing into the feet of a statue:

> *You watched while a stone was cut out without hands, which struck the image on its feet of iron and clay, and broke them in pieces. Then the iron, the clay, the bronze, the silver, and the gold were crushed together, and became like chaff from the summer threshing floors; the wind carried them away so that no trace of them was found. And the stone that struck the image became a great mountain and filled the whole earth. (Daniel 2:34, 35)*

The stone was "cut out without hands." In other words, human beings would not usher in the Kingdom of Christ; God Himself would. In later years, when Christians staged an uprising and resorted to violence in the streets of Wittenberg, Martin Luther rebuked them by appealing to the same passage from Daniel: "Remember," he told the angry mobs, "that Antichrist, as Daniel said, is to be broken without the hand of man. Violence will only make him stronger. Preach, pray, but do not fight."[9]

While there have always been Christians who ignored the teachings of Jesus, the likelihood that 1st century Christians burned down the city of Rome to hasten the Second Coming was highly unlikely. But in the face of a crisis, facts seldom matter to the anxious. The Christians received the blame, and Nero, relieved to be out of the spotlight, went after them with a horrific ferocity.

Christians were falsely accused of the most dreadful crimes and declared to be the cause of great calamities—famine, pestilence, and earthquake. As the followers of the Nazarene became the objects of popular hatred and suspicion, informers stood ready, for the sake of gain, to betray the innocent to the authorities. They were condemned as rebels against the empire—as foes of religion and pests to society. Their very existence in Rome brought disfavor from the gods.

Great numbers of Christians were thrown to wild beasts or burned alive in the amphitheaters. Some were crucified; others were covered with the skins of wild animals and thrust into the arena to be torn apart by dogs. Their punishment was often made the chief entertainment at public fetes. Vast multitudes assembled to enjoy the sight and greeted their dying agonies with laughter and applause.

A Roman historian named Tacitus, who lived in that era and was no fan of Nero, wrote about the emperor's efforts to quash the rumor that *he* had ordered the fire:

> But all human efforts, all the lavish gifts of the emperor, and the propitiations of the gods, did not banish the sinister belief that the conflagration was the result of an order. Consequently, to get rid of the report, Nero fastened the guilt and inflicted the most exquisite tortures on a class hated for their abominations, called Christians by the populace. Christus, from whom the name had its origin, suffered the extreme penalty during

the reign of Tiberius at the hands of one of our procurators, Pontius Pilatus, and a most mischievous superstition, thus checked for the moment, again broke out not only in Judaea, the first source of the evil, but even in Rome, where all things hideous and shameful from every part of the world find their centre and become popular. Accordingly, an arrest was first made of all who pleaded guilty; then, upon their information, an immense multitude was convicted, not so much of the crime of firing the city, as of hatred against mankind. Mockery of every sort was added to their deaths. Covered with the skins of beasts, they were torn by dogs and perished, or were nailed to crosses, or were doomed to the flames and burnt, to serve as a nightly illumination, when daylight had expired.

Nero offered his gardens for the spectacle, and was exhibiting a show in the circus, while he mingled with the people in the dress of a charioteer or stood aloft on a car. Hence, even for criminals who deserved extreme and exemplary punishment, there arose a feeling of compassion; for it was not, as it seemed, for the public good, but to glut one man's cruelty, that they were being destroyed.[10]

The Christians may not have been the emperor's first target, according to some historians. It is suggested that Nero initially blamed another easy target, the poor, because he knew that nobody would defend them. Among the poor, however, there were lots of Christians, because from the start it was the religion of a poor carpenter's Son—the religion of outcasts and the downtrodden. Christianity was a movement started by a Man who spent time with tax collectors, lepers, and prostitutes.

In its earliest days, Christianity was not the religion of the rich and wealthy.

However, when poor Christians were faced with execution, they died so fearlessly that people took note. Their bravery set them apart, which drew more attention to them, and eventually made them the number-one scapegoat—the face of all the emperor's problems. The problems for Christians multiplied as the years went by, and before long, everybody knew they didn't fit the empire. Jesus was not welcome in the highest levels of Roman society. There was no room for Him, not only at the inn of Bethlehem, but also not in the emperor's palace.

The problems ran deeper than mere cultural differences. As Romans became more aware of Christian doctrine, they began to mount serious philosophical opposition—much of it centered around the fact that Christians revered Jesus of Nazareth as God in human flesh—a big no-no to their way of thinking.

The concept of the God-man, the divinity of Christ, has always been a lightning rod for the critics of Christianity. In recent years, some have argued that the doctrine of Christ's divinity was actually a later development, imported into the church by Constantine the Great. One of the more notable examples from popular literature (as opposed to scholarly work) can be found in Dan Brown's best-selling novel, *The Da Vinci Code*:

> *"Fortunately for historians," Teabing said, "some of the gospels that Constantine attempted to eradicate managed to survive. The Dead Sea Scrolls were found in the 1950s hidden in a cave near Qumran in the Judean desert. And, of course, the Coptic Scrolls in 1945 at Nag Hammadi. In addition to telling the*

true Grail story, these documents speak of Christ's ministry in very human terms. Of course, the Vatican, in keeping with their tradition of misinformation, tried very hard to suppress the release of these scrolls. And why wouldn't they? The scrolls highlight glaring historical discrepancies and fabrications, clearly confirming that the modern Bible was compiled and edited by men who possessed a political agenda—to promote the divinity of the man Jesus Christ and use His influence to solidify their own power base."[11]

Serious historians and biblical scholars decried Dan Brown's theory as utter fiction, and for good reason. The New Testament, authored more than two centuries before the rise of Constantine, makes clear reference to Jesus' divinity:

In the beginning was the Word, and the Word was with God, and the Word was God. He was in the beginning with God. All things were made through Him, and without Him nothing was made that was made. (John 1:1-3)

Therefore the Jews sought all the more to kill Him, because He not only broke the Sabbath, but also said that God was His Father, making Himself equal with God. (John 5:18)

But when He again brings the firstborn into the world, He says: "Let all the angels of God worship Him." (Hebrews 1:6)

Of course, critics would defer to the notion that Constantine essentially hand-picked which books would appear in the New Testament (another bit of fiction, as we will discover), but the fact remains that the Gospel of John and the book of Hebrews originate from the 1st century, not the 4th.

Roman philosophical opposition to Christian doctrine provides further proof that Christians worshipped Jesus as God right from the beginning. In the last half of the 2nd century, a harsh Roman critic named Celsus took the Christians to task. Celsus' attacks were enough that Christians felt obliged to respond to him. The reason we know what Celsus said, in fact, is because the apologist Origen of Alexandria's thorough rebuttal is still in existence.

One of Celsus' criticisms was built on the Christian doctrine of the incarnation, the notion that God had become a flesh-and-blood human being in the person of Jesus of Nazareth. According to him, for God to debase Himself—to change from good to bad, from beautiful to shameful—was outrageous. A bona fide god simply wouldn't humble himself to that extent.

Of course, typical of Roman pragmatic thinkers, he failed to understand that the condescension of God was an act of *agape* love, the emptying of one's self for the sake of others.

In addition to the incarnation, Celsus also attacked the divinity of Christ on another front. A number of prominent pagan thinkers had been moving away from *polytheism,* the idea that there are many gods, toward *monotheism,* the teaching that there is only one. In this, they were following in the footsteps of some earlier Greek thinkers who had become so embarrassed by the capricious behavior of their pantheon that they had begun shying away from it. Writing some 500 years before Christ, Xenophanes of Colophon, for example, had declared, "God is one, supreme among gods and men, and not like mortals in body or in mind."[12] Polytheism was falling out of fashion among intellectuals, and as far as Celsus was concerned, the divinity of Christ was an anti-intellectual relapse, a return to many gods.

He also took exception to the resurrection of Christ. People simply do not rise from the dead, yet Christians were adamant that Jesus had returned from the grave, and they staked their entire belief system on it. Paul had written that if Jesus did *not* rise from the dead, then there was no point to the Christian faith, and no hope for the future:

> For if the dead do not rise, then Christ is not risen. And if Christ is not risen, your faith is futile; you are still in your sins! Then also those who have fallen asleep in Christ have perished. If in this life only we have hope in Christ, we are of all men the most pitiable. But now Christ is risen from the dead, and has become the firstfruits of those who have fallen asleep. For since by man came death, by Man also came the resurrection of the dead. For as in Adam all die, even so in Christ all shall be made alive. But each one in his own order: Christ the firstfruits, afterward those who are Christ's at His coming. Then comes the end, when He delivers the kingdom to God the Father, when He puts an end to all rule and all authority and power. (1 Corinthians 15:16-24)

The Christian hope of a coming Kingdom was based entirely on the belief that Jesus had conquered death and would eventually return for His church. When one among their number died, they were instructed to speak of the coming resurrection made possible by the resurrection of Christ:

But I do not want you to be ignorant, brethren, concerning those who have fallen asleep, lest you sorrow as others who have no hope. For if we believe that Jesus died and rose again, even so God will bring with Him those who sleep in Jesus. For this we say to you by the word of the Lord, that we who are alive and remain until the coming of the Lord will by no means precede those who are asleep. For the Lord Himself will descend from heaven with a shout, with the voice of an archangel, and with the trumpet of God. And the dead in Christ will rise first. Then we who are alive and remain shall be caught up together with them in the clouds to meet the Lord in the air. And thus we shall always be with the Lord. Therefore comfort one another with these words. (1 Thessalonians 4:13-18)

Celsus found the idea nonsensical and ridiculed the Christians over it: the dead do *not* come back to life.

Of course, if the divinity of Christ had been a later addition to Christian belief, introduced by Constantine in the 4th century, it leaves one to wonder what Celsus was protesting against roughly 150 years earlier.

After Celsus, another pagan philosopher named Porphyry took exception to Christians, calling them unsophisticated simpletons who were holding back the progress of civilization—a charge still leveled against Christians by modern critics like Richard Dawkins. In Porphyry's opinion, Christians were standing in the way of the advancement of logic and science.

In the first three centuries of the church's existence, Christians faced opposition on many fronts: social, political, religious, and philosophical. They didn't have many supporters, and in the

Roman world, the worth of Jesus would have to be proved.

On that front, Constantine had something in common with Jesus: he would have to prove *his* worth to the Roman Empire. It wasn't until his father's cape suddenly came out of storage that Helena was able to prove that her boy was important. And even though they were separated by nearly three centuries, the paths of Jesus of Nazareth and Constantine of Naissus were destined to cross—and when they did, the impact on Western civilization was huge. It changed the world so much that we continue to live in Constantine's shadow.

It leads us to an important question, one that lingers to this day: when it did happen, was the intersection of Jesus and Constantine a good thing, or did Constantine actually hinder the progress of the cause of Christ for many centuries to come?

FOOTNOTES FOR CHAPTER TWO

6. Shakespeare, William. *Julius Caesar.* New Haven: Yale University Press, 1964. Print, 8-9.

7. "Encyclopaedia Judaica: Birkat Ha-Minim." Jewish Virtual Library. Digital.

8. Potter, D. S. *The Roman Empire at Bay: AD 180-395.* London: Routledge, 2004. Print, 241.

9. Bainton, Roland H. *Here I Stand: A Life of Martin Luther.* New York: Abingdon-Cokesbury, 1950. Print, 205.

10. Tacitus, Cornelius. *Annals, Book XV,* Ch. 44. Translation by Alfred John Church. London, 1876. Print.

11. Brown, Dan. *The Da Vinci Code.* New York: Doubleday, 2003. Digital, 254-255.

12. Xenophanes, *Fragments, No. 1.*

CHAPTER THREE

Most people consider the city of Rome to be the capital of the Roman Empire, and with good reason. The empire was born in this city of Romulus and Remus and expanded from there. Rome was the home of Julius Caesar and the Senate. But in later years, the locus of power shifted from west to east, and the capital moved across the Bosphorus to Asia Minor, which roughly corresponds to modern-day Turkey. In fact, long after the western part of the empire collapsed in the late 5th century, it continued to thrive in the east.

Asia Minor was also home to the Christian community, which quickly spread from Jerusalem. By the time John wrote the book of Revelation, toward the end of the 1st century, there were vibrant churches in most of the key cities of Asia Minor. Tradition has it that when John was sent to a penal colony on Patmos, he may have been the pastor of the Christian community in Ephesus, one of the seven churches mentioned in the opening chapters of the book of Revelation.

Over the years, Bible students have found an interesting pattern in the letters addressed to the seven churches of Asia Minor, found in the second and third chapters of Revelation. They were originally addressed to real congregations in the 1st century, and they deal with real issues that existed at the time, but the intent of each message seems to run much deeper.

Any time the number seven shows up in Bible prophecy, it's usually significant. Seven is highly symbolic: it is the number of completeness or perfection. God's perfect creation, after all, was accomplished in six days, and then He rested on the seventh, bringing the creation story to perfect completion.

It is interesting that there are messages for precisely seven churches, even though we know there were more Christian communities in Asia Minor at the time. (For example, there was a sizable congregation at Colossae, to which Paul's letter to the Colossians was addressed, but they failed to make the list in Revelation.) A list of seven indicates a symbolic meaning, so the reader should dig deeper than what is on the surface alone.

For centuries, students of the book of Revelation have strongly suspected that the seven churches also represent the entire history of Christianity, from the earliest days of the church until the Second Coming of Christ. It is the complete story of Christian history, written in advance.

The first letter is addressed to the church in Ephesus, the group of believers in John's home. And while the content of the letter appears to address local issues at the time, it also seems to point to 1st century Christianity as a whole—a time when the church was still being led by people who had known Jesus personally (see Revelation 2:1-7). The letter serves as a warning that the early church was in danger of leaving its first love. (Revelation 2:4)

The second letter is addressed to the people of Smyrna, a city whose very name implies something being crushed. "Smyrna" is virtually synonymous with the word "myrrh," which was one of the gifts the wise men brought to the infant Jesus. (Matthew 2:11) It was a sweet-smelling fragrance obtained by crushing the myrrh plant. Before you could enjoy the rich fragrance of the plant, you had to brutally destroy it.

The letter to Smyrna appears to be addressed to people who would suffer severe persecution; in fact, many modern English editions of the Bible have inserted a section heading over the letter to Smyrna that reads, "The Persecuted Church." (See, for example, the subtitles in New King James Version of the book of Revelation.)

It corresponds to the second phase of the church's experience: life under Roman persecution. As the Romans saw the Christian church as a threat to the empire's stability, they began to put pressure on the church; in effect, they attempted to crush it.

As we saw in the previous chapter, a fire left about 70 percent of Rome burned to the ground, and the Christians were blamed because they spoke of the end of the world with fire. From that point forward, Christians started meeting with especially cruel and painful deaths.

During this time, under Nero, the Apostle Paul was beheaded outside of Rome, likely in the location now marked by the Three Fountains Abbey. (There are three springs under the church at the abbey. An apocryphal story states that when Paul's head hit the ground, it hit the ground three times, and each time it did, a spring of water erupted from the ground.)

It was also during this time that Peter was locked in a dark musty cell at the bottom of the Mamertine Prison. He was later led outside of the city—likely to the spot now marked by the Vatican—and crucified upside-down. (If you visit the Mamertine Prison today, you'll find a small altar in the cell marked with an inverted cross. Occasionally, poorly-informed conspiracy theorists attempt to suggest that it is a satanic symbol, but it is simply a reflection of the story of Peter's martyrdom.) Why was Peter crucified upside-down? It's because he didn't feel worthy to be executed in the same manner as Jesus:

> *Among many other saints, the blessed apostle Peter was con-*
> *demned to death, and crucified, as some do write, at Rome;*
> *albeit some others, and not without cause, do doubt thereof.*
> *Hegesippus saith that Nero sought matter against Peter to put*
> *him to death; which, when the people perceived, they entreated*
> *Peter with much ado that he would fly the city. Peter, through*
> *their importunity at length persuaded, prepared himself to*
> *avoid. But, coming to the gate, he saw the Lord Christ come to*
> *meet him, to whom he, worshipping, said, "Lord, whither dost*
> *Thou go?" To whom He answered and said, "I am come*
> *again to be crucified." By this, Peter, perceiving his suffering to*
> *be understood, returned into the city. Jerome saith that he was*
> *crucified, his head being down and his feet upward, himself so*
> *requiring, because he was (he said) unworthy to be crucified*
> *after the same form and manner as the Lord was.*[13]

Jesus had, in fact, warned Peter about his manner of death ahead of time, when He predicted: "Most assuredly, I say to you, when you were younger, you girded yourself and walked where you wished; but when you are old, you will stretch out your hands, and another will gird you and carry you where you do not wish." (John 21:18)

It was a difficult time for Christians, to say the least, and many Bible students recognize a special message encoded in Revelation's letter to Smyrna from Christ to those who would live through Roman persecution:

And to the angel of the church in Smyrna write, "These things says the First and the Last, who was dead, and came to life: 'I know your works, tribulation, and poverty but you are rich; and I know the blasphemy of those who say they are Jews and are not, but are a synagogue of Satan. Do not fear any of those things which you are about to suffer. Indeed, the devil is about to throw some of you into prison, that you may be tested, and you will have tribulation ten days. Be faithful until death, and I will give you the crown of life. He who has an ear, let him hear what the Spirit says to the churches. He who overcomes shall not be hurt by the second death.'" (Revelation 2:8-11)

Notice the troubling themes of the letter: death, suffering, prison, tribulation. It is a message from One who had already suffered and been executed at the hands of the Romans, a Man who had been condemned in a Roman court and died on a Roman cross. It offers reassurance and hope to those who would suffer a similar fate.

It also makes cryptic reference to a special period of suffering that would last 10 days. In the language of Bible prophecy, 10 "days" is most likely a symbolic reference to 10 literal years. (In Ezekiel 4:6, for example, God instructs Ezekiel to lie on his side for 40 days, one day for each year that Judah had rebelled against Him. In Daniel 9, the prophecy of 70 weeks, or 490 days, is widely believed to refer to 490 years, and suddenly becomes stunningly accurate when considered that way.)

The letter to Smyrna predicts 10 years of heightened persecution, which, remarkably, is exactly what happened. The story of the 10-year persecution proves to be a prediction of Constantine, and provides a key point where the stories of Jesus and Constantine begin to merge.

It's an amazing story.

On the battlefields of the empire, something incredible took place. In AD 284, near the modern-day city of İzmit, in Turkey, the commander of the imperial bodyguard was suddenly declared to be emperor by his troops. His name was Diocletian (b. Diocles), and his rise to the emperor's chair was very unusual.

One year before Diocletian came to power, the emperor Carus suddenly died while fighting against the Persians. Some think that he had a heart attack; it was said that he died "as if he were struck by a thunderbolt." Before his death, his two sons had already been made Caesars, which was a kind of vice-emperor. Carus was trying to build a family dynasty, one that would continue long after his demise.

Upon Carus' untimely death, one son was given control of the west, and the other was given control of the east. The son who inherited the west was named Carinus, after his father. He controlled the region comprised of Gaul (roughly corresponding to today's France), Spain, the British Isles, and North Africa along the Mediterranean coast. Unfortunately, Carinus was a cruel, licentious man given to violence and debauchery. One account tells us that when Carinus reached the city of Rome, "he executed the city's Prefect and replaced him with Matronianus, a crony of his and a procurer who had always served him in his debaucheries… By frequent marriage and divorce he took nine wives altogether and threw some of them away even while they were pregnant. He filled the palaces with actors, pantomimes, harlots, singers and procurers."[14]

His self-serving lifestyle eventually caught up with him: one of his own soldiers, enraged over Carinus' rape of his wife, took advantage of the fog of war and literally stabbed the Caesar in the back.

Carus' other son, Numerian, inherited control of the east. He, too, died an untimely death, and it has long been suspected that Diocletian orchestrated it.

The story was told that Numerian had an eye infection, which was aggravated by dust and sunlight, so he had to spend his days riding inside a litter—a hand-carried carriage—in order to protect his eye. For a while, the story made sense, until people began to wonder why he *never* emerged, not even to answer the call of nature.

Eventually, a slave opened the door to the litter to discover the dead body of Numerian.

Numerian's death created a problem for Diocles, the commander of the *Protectores Domestici:* he was responsible for the emperor's safety. If the emperor was dead, it was his sworn duty to find the perpetrator and bring him to justice.

Like a good Roman, he found a scapegoat: Numerian's father-in-law, Lucius Aper. In the middle of the night, Diocles went into Lucius' tent and had him arrested. He gathered his legion commanders around door of the tent, where he dumped the badly decomposing body of Numerian on the ground in front of them.

"You did this," he said, pointing to Lucius.

Of course, Lucius denied it, so they put him on trial on the spot.

Diocles made a speech in front of all the soldiers: "For the past four days," he said, "legion commanders have been asking

Lucius Aper to arrange a meeting with the emperor. Their requests were denied. I, the commander of the *Protectores Domestici*, asked Lucius Aper about the emperor's health. I was told that he was suffering from an ailment of the eyes. I did not become suspicious until a faithful soldier reported to me that for days the emperor had not left the litter even to relieve himself."[15]

And at the end of the speech, he pointed straight at Lucius Aper: "HE is the murderer!"

Of course, Lucius responded in anger, indicting Diocles. "*He* is the murderer," he cried, "not me! Are you going to believe the words of a plotter, the words of a filthy son of a slave?"

It was more than an accusation; it was an outright insult, the last straw for Diocles. He pulled out a knife and stabbed Lucius on the spot, after which his men unanimously declared him the new emperor. One of the Roman commanders, a man named Valerius Maximianus, a trusted colleague of Diocles, climbed atop a small hill and, before the soldiers could get over the shock of what had just happened, proclaimed: "Romans, this is a moment of destiny. The future of Rome is in the hands of her legions. Hail the Augustus, Hail Gaius, Aurelius, Valerius Diocletianus, Dominus, Pontifex Maximus, Restorer and Protector." Before long, all the soldiers began to shout, "Hail Augustus Diocletianus!"

Diocles became Diocletian, the new emperor of Rome.

It was a big job, with a lot of responsibility. Keeping the empire stable and united was a gargantuan task. The Roman territories were huge, comprised of most of today's France, Spain, England, Switzerland, Italy, the Balkans, Greece, Turkey, Israel, Lebanon, Jordan, Syria, Egypt, and North Africa. It was an empire made up of many diverse people, with widely divergent faiths, cultures, languages, and loyalties.

And all of them had been conquered.

The empire was difficult to control, especially for one man who could only be in one place at a time. Diocletian did something ingenious: in AD 283, he divided responsibility among four men, creating a *tetrarchy*. In the east, there would be two emperors: a senior emperor, known as an *Augustus*, and a junior emperor, known as *Caesar*. The same would be true for the west.

Naturally, in the east, Diocletian became the Augustus, and he appointed a Caesar by the name of Galerius. In the west, Maximian was appointed Augustus, and his junior, the Caesar, was the powerful governor of Dalmatia, Flavius Constantius, the father of Constantine.

As soon as Constantine's father was promoted, he moved his family to the city of Arelate, corresponding to Arles in modern-day France. The promotion meant a lot of changes for Flavius Constantius, not the least of which was the sudden need to be rid of his substandard wife, Helena.

He divorced her.

Helena was a commoner, a concubine, and of course, that wouldn't do for a Caesar. Diocletian pressured Constantius to get rid of her and upgrade to a more suitable spouse: the daughter of his senior emperor, Maximian. Her name was Theodora, and she was 26 years his junior.

The divorce and remarriage was a political move, calculated to strengthen the bonds of the tetrarchy. In the east, he had Galerius do the same thing: divorce his current wife and marry Diocletian's daughter. Betrayal, after all, becomes much more difficult when the person you're betraying is a relative.

One can only imagine the heartache Helena suffered when she received the news that she was to be replaced by a younger woman, a member of Roman high society. Her past, it seems, would always be an obstacle to full acceptance.

It is at this point that many historians believe that Helena stepped completely outside of Roman custom and turned to the Christian faith in order to find comfort. If she did, the implications are staggering, to say the least. A member of one of the highest-ranking households in the empire now belonged to a sect the empire hated with a passion. Like other Romans who had turned to Christ before her, Helena had a humble background, but her conversion was different: the faith of Jesus had just found a home in the highest circles of Roman civilization.

Constantine was also deeply impacted by his father's promotion and subsequent rejection of his mother. While history provides no details, many believe (quite reasonably) that he harbored resentment for the rest of his life. He was now a grown man, and he was suddenly sent east to Asia Minor to work for Diocletian. He was given a post in the imperial guard in the city of Nicomedia, which corresponds to present-day İznik in Turkey. Young Constantine became a centurion, living full-time with the emperor and traveling with him across the empire for about a dozen years:

> For the next 12 years Constantine was to be a member of that strange institution, the "sacred retinue," the migratory capital of the empire. Diocletian was perpetually on the move, inspecting the frontiers, reviewing the administration of the provinces and suppressing occasional revolts.[16]

Diocletian's methods and style of government undoubtedly shaped the young Constantine. If you spend that much time in close contact with the emperor, something's bound to rub off on you. Constantine likely learned much of his own management style from Diocletian, one of the most notorious emperors in history.

The other thing that is bound to rub off on you when you live in close contact with the emperor is the impression that his divinity is exaggerated. One can only imagine just how *human* Diocletian must have seemed to young Constantine, especially knowing that the emperor had ordered the dissolution of his mother's marriage.

In hindsight, it is obvious that Constantine's time with Diocletian was formative, and likely fueled his own ambition. He was, after all, the son of a Caesar.

Even with the division of his empire into a tetrarchy, Diocletian continued to face threats to the empire's stability, and early on, he was forced to deal with a serious one. A religious sect known as the Manicheans emerged in Egypt, a group founded by a Persian prophet named Mani. The prophet taught that salvation was to be found in education and fasting and by living an ascetic, self-denying life. The religion spread quickly, and at its height, Manichean churches and writings could be found as far east as China.

Unfortunately for the Christians, Mani generated confusion about their faith, because he borrowed heavily from the doctrines of the Christian church. Though not an adherent of the Christian church, he declared himself to be an apostle of Christ—in spite of the fact that he promoted beliefs at odds with Christianity, such as reincarnation. The prophet was also a fan of Buddha, Zoroaster, and Krishna, and had no problem amalgamating their teachings with those of Jesus.

Mani was not a Christian, but that didn't matter to the Romans, because they didn't care what people believed. If someone wanted to believe what Mani taught, that was of no consequence—unless you did what the Egyptian Manicheans did. They staged a revolt. Manicheans, together with the Greek aristocracy in Egypt, had never fully accepted Roman rule, and when they thought the time was right, they attempted to liberate themselves. They rose up and suddenly overran one Roman garrison after another.

At that point, their religious beliefs suddenly became a *big* issue.

Diocletian *had* to take action. He marched into Egypt to put an end to the rebellion. He became convinced that the Manicheans were more than a domestic threat. Someone suggested that the Persian king had planted the sect in Egypt in order to destabilize the empire. He had no choice but to brutally squash the movement, and he literally sent the Manicheans to the salt mines.

Constantine, now 25 years old, was there.

It was a disturbing foreshadowing of how the empire was about to deal with Christians. As far as the Romans were concerned, there was crucial link between Manicheanism and Christianity. Mani, after all, had declared himself to be an apostle of Christ, and he taught a number of things that closely paralleled Christianity: the promise of an eternal reward in the afterlife, redemption from sin, and justification before God. The religions of Rome didn't offer such things; most Romans paid obeisance to the pagan gods in the hopes that the gods would simply leave them alone. Unfortunately for the Christian community, Mani appeared to be offering the same things Jesus did, and to the mind of the average Roman, there was little difference.

In the beginning, it didn't really affect the Christians. There was a Christian church in Nicomedia, the capital of Diocletian's empire, proof that Christians were relatively free in the early years of his reign, and the emperor didn't consider them a threat.

His junior, Caesar Galerius, thought otherwise. In AD 302, Galerius began to complain that the Christians in Nicomedia were offending the Romans by disregarding the traditional Roman gods. If someone disrespected the Roman gods, he asserted, it was akin to disrespecting the Roman emperor.

By this time, some Christians had risen from the lower strata of Roman society into more responsible positions in the empire, and as a result, they became more exposed to Roman religion, and the public became more exposed to *them*. Since the emperor was considered to be the son of a god, or one of the gods, Christian disregard for the Roman pantheon could be interpreted as a rejection of the emperor himself.

Galerius' mother, Romula, had come to Nicomedia from modern-day Bulgaria. She was a pagan priestess who discovered that Christians were not interested in her pagan rituals, and it angered her. The ancient Christian writer Lactantius describes what happened:

> *The mother of Galerius, a woman exceedingly superstitious, was a votary of the gods of the mountains. Being of such a character, she made sacrifices almost every day, and she feasted her servants on the meat offered to idols: but the Christians of her family would not partake of those entertainments; and while she feasted with the Gentiles, they continued in fasting and prayer. On this account she conceived ill-will against the*

*Christians, and by woman-like complaints instigated her son,
no less superstitious than herself, to destroy them.*[17]

The Christians, she suggested, were offending the traditional gods, and she instructed Galerius to go after them. Word went from Galerius to Diocletian. He started to suggest to the Augustus that if the Christians were not dealt with, it could spell trouble for the empire.

At about the same time, the pagan philosopher Porphyry began to publish against the Christians. Porphyry, an educated man, suggested that the Christian rejection of Rome's traditional gods posed a threat to the stability of the empire, because it weakened the fabric—the glue—that traditionally held society together. His writings were so influential that Christians continued to feel the need to answer his charges long after his death.

(In fact, Porphyry's writings were so influential that eventually some of his suggestions made it *into* the Christian religion. Perhaps most famously, he attacked the book of Daniel, which presents powerful evidence for the existence of the Judeo-Christian God. Porphyry suggested that, given the stunning accuracy of the predictions in Daniel, it must have been written at a later date, after the events had taken place. Rejecting the claims of the author, he argued that Daniel was written in the 2nd century BC, well after the Babylonian and Persian Empires. Rather than Daniel, a group of Jews under siege from the Seleucid Greeks had written the book. Unfortunately, that opinion, authored by a dedicated critic of Christianity, has managed to make its way into significant number of modern commentaries. Higher critics will often suggest that the book of Daniel was written at a much later date, around 167-164 BC, during the Maccabean revolt against Antiochus Epiphanes. Daniel's history, it is said, is *vaticinia ex eventu*, a Latin phrase for "written after the happening took place." However, even if one *did* assume that it was written in the 160s BC, how could anyone living more than 150 years before the birth of Christ accurately predict the dismantling of the Roman Empire—an event that took place in AD 476? Daniel accurately depicted the fragmentation of the Western Roman Empire into pieces that would never "cleave one to another, even as iron is not mixed with clay," rightly predicting that, in spite of herculean efforts, nobody would be able to repair the Roman Empire.)

Porphyry's attacks had a negative effect on the church. When you combined the writings of Porphyry with the hatred of Galerius and his mother, and you added the apparent similarities of Manichaeism, you suddenly had a renewed discomfort with the Christian religion. The Christians had enjoyed a pretty good life for almost 50 years without serious persecution. For the first 17 years of Diocletian's reign, he was so busy securing the empire that he never really thought about the Christians. He obviously knew they existed, but the only thing he really knew about them was that Christian soldiers obeyed his orders, just like everybody else. But after the Manichean revolt, and the complaints of Galerius, he started to suspect that maybe the Christians were a problem after all. The heat was rising, and with a junior emperor eager to get rid of the followers of Jesus, something was bound to happen.

In September, AD 302, Diocletian went to visit frontier garrisons in the Balkans. Because of Galerius' insistence that Christians were a problem, he started to ask questions. Everybody he asked—commanders, civilian administrators, the locals—all told him the same thing: Christians were good citizens and faithful soldiers.

They did have one complaint, however—the same complaint that followed Christians wherever they went in the empire: they wouldn't participate in public sacrifices to the Roman gods. To the Roman way of thinking, their refusal could become a significant problem because the Roman gods might get offended and quit helping on the battlefield. The refusal of Christian troops to participate made the pagan soldiers nervous.

"Their numbers are growing," someone told the emperor. "The army is *full* of these Christians, and so is the civil list. Their first loyalty is to a crucified Jew they address as *Dominus*, claiming that He is the Lord and Savior."[18]

That of course, *did* bother the emperor. He had been working hard to unify a massive empire, and there were soldiers whose highest loyalty belonged to someone else—a Jew who had been crucified by Pontius Pilate.

In October of AD 302, he called a meeting of high-ranking officials, and he got more disturbing news. A man by the name of Hierocles, the governor of Bithynia, said, "Do not think that this cult is like the cult of Mithras. The followers of Mithras never spoke against the Roman gods, but the Christians consider OUR gods to be demons, unholy spirits, and they claim that the Hebrew rebel they worship is the only true God."

It wasn't good news for Diocletian, yet he found himself reluctant to use violence against the Christians. Other than their peculiar religious beliefs, the Christians had proven to be good citizens, and that was important in Rome. He also knew that violence doesn't tend to encourage continued loyalty. It might help stop an insurrection, but as a preemptive measure, violence tended to sow anger and resentment, and might actually pave the way toward outright rebellion—precisely what he hoped to avoid.

He also knew, from history, that if he attempted to kill Christians, they would voluntarily march to their deaths. They would become martyrs before they would give up their faith in Jesus and worship the Roman gods. The past had also proven that the more these people had been persecuted, the more they grew in numbers, and that would only make his problem worse.

Diocletian decided to start with civil penalties. He dismissed all the Christians from his army, and fired the Christians who worked in his palace. Just to be sure he was doing the right thing, he sent a messenger to the famous Oracle at Didyma, in order to ask the god Apollo what *he* thought:

> *About that time it is said that Apollo spoke from a deep and gloomy cavern, and through the medium of no human voice, and declared that the righteous men on earth were a bar to his speaking the truth, and accordingly that the oracles from the tripod were fallacious.*[19]

In other words, Apollo had nothing to say. Why? The presence of the "righteous men on earth" were preventing him from speaking. Diocletian was on his own.

That was bad news. Who were these righteous ones standing in the way of Apollo's help? In later years, Constantine recounted Diocletian's distress with the church historian Eusebius:

> *I heard him who at that time was chief among the Roman emperors, unhappy, truly unhappy as he was, and laboring*

under mental delusion, make earnest enquiry of his atten-
dants as to who these righteous ones on earth were, and that
one of the Pagan priests then present replied that they were
doubtless the Christians. This answer he eagerly received,
like some honeyed draught, and unsheathed the sword which
was ordained for the punishment of crime, against those
whose holiness was beyond reproach. Immediately, therefore,
he issued those sanguinary edicts, traced, if I may so express
myself, with a sword's point dipped in blood; at the same time
commanding his judges to tax their ingenuity for the inven-
tion of new and more terrible punishments.[20]

Something had to be done, and where Diocletian had previously been hesitant, he finally let loose his fury against the
sect of Christians. On February 23 in AD 303, soldiers suddenly
stormed the Christian church in Nicomedia. They knocked
down the building with a battering ram and burned all the
books. Galerius actually wanted to burn the church itself, but
Diocletian stopped him, afraid that a fire might endanger the
whole city. By the end of the day, the battering ram had been
worked hard, and the church was nothing but a pile of rubble.

Dark times were, indeed, coming for the children of Light.

The next day, the Roman government posted a public edict
against Christians. It was copied and sent throughout the realm.
Both Maximian and Constantius were ordered to implement
the edict in their territories as well.

Christians were suddenly denied their religious liberty.
They no longer had a right to worship. Their church buildings
were to be torn down. Their Scriptures were to be confiscated
and burned publicly. They were to be denied the protection of

law: if someone attacked a Christian or robbed him, they could do it with impunity and keep what they stole. Christians were now non-persons.

A few months later, the leaders of the church were rounded up and told that if they didn't offer sacrifices to the emperor, they would be put to death.

The same day the authorities posted the edict, a Christian by the name of Euethius lost his temper and ripped the edict down:

> *The very same day the imperial edict was posted in Nicomedia, a zealot Christian, a young man by the name of Euethius, tore down the parchment and tramped it on the ground shouting in front of onlookers: "Here are your Gothic and Sarmatian triumphs," referring tauntingly to Diocletian's titles "Gothicus" and "Sarmaticus" which had been bestowed on him after his victories over those barbarian tribes. The young man was immediately arrested by the home guards, the scutarii, and taken to a judicial magistrate. We have enough information to reconstruct the scene. The judge listened as one of the guards described the incident, then he turned to the prisoner.*
>
> *"Is this all true?" he asked.*
> *"Yes, it is," Euethius replied defiantly.*
> *"You admit that you insulted the sacred person of the Augustus?"*
> *"For me, only the person of Christ is sacred."*
> *"If I condemn you, it will not be for your religion; it will be for your insolent act against the emperor."[21]*

The judge attempted to defend religious liberty, something the Romans cared about, because they knew that to maintain stability in the empire, the people needed to be able to practice their own faiths. Again, the Romans didn't care about Christianity as a religion; what they *truly* cared about was political stability. It's the reason they crucified Christ: they were told that He was claiming to be another king. Remember the sign that Pilate posted above Jesus' head: "Jesus of Nazareth, the King of the Jews." (John 19:19) The Romans didn't care what Jesus taught or believed; they cared only that He was perceived to be a threat to the political stability of the region and, hence, the empire (a revolt in one place tended to lead to revolts in other places).

After the judge spoke, Euethius answered, "I insulted the emperor only because he insulted my Lord and Savior. If you kill me, you will not give me death but life eternal. I pity you."

"You are an idiot," the judge said, "but the law does not exempt idiots from just punishment. Take him away. Torture him and then burn him on the stake."[22]

Guards took Euethius, hung him on an iron hook and whipped him all night long. When the sun rose in the morning, they tied him to a stake and burned him to death.

"He suffered death," wrote one historian, "with admirable patience."

Diocletian was not happy with the Euethius incident. He really didn't want to kill Christians—he merely hoped to make life miserable enough that they would come to their senses and offer sacrifices to the gods.

It would never happen. Such acts, the Christians believed, could cost them eternal life. They followed in the footsteps of those who had defied such orders in the past, courageous individuals like Shadrach, Meschach, and Abednego. When faced with death threats, they still refused to bow before Nebuchadnezzar's idol. "O Nebuchadnezzar," they replied, "we have no need to answer you in this matter. If that is the case, our God whom we serve is able to deliver us from the burning fiery furnace, and He will deliver us from your hand, O king. But if not, let it be known to you, O king, that we do not serve your gods, nor will we worship the gold image which you have set up." (Daniel 3:16-18)

Euethius was the first victim of the infamous Diocletian persecution, and he might have been the last, except for something that happened a few weeks later: someone started a fire in Diocletian's palace. It started on the ground floor, near the slave quarters. The resulting inferno was serious enough that both Diocletian and Galerius had to flee that part of the building, dressed only in their nightclothes. The wing where Diocletian and his family lived was all but destroyed.

Today, some historians believe that Galerius started the fire himself in an attempt to strengthen Diocletian's resolve against the Christians—much the way Nero had burned Rome and framed the Christians. It worked remarkably well in the 1st century; why not try it again?

Diocletian continued to exercise caution. He wanted to find out the truth before he started blaming anyone for the arson. A number of slaves were arrested and tortured on the rack in order to extract information, but the slaves revealed nothing because, most likely, they knew nothing.

In order to convince the emperor to act, Galerius needed further proof that the Christians were to blame, so he hatched a rather ingenious plan. He planned a public ceremony in order to thank the Roman gods for sparing the emperor's family. Knowing, of course, that the Christians would not participate, he set a trap for them. Anyone who didn't participate, he suggested, was likely displeased with the emperor's survival, and was obviously responsible for the crime.

Diocletian approved of the plan, and called for the priests of Jupiter to organize a public sacrifice. Everyone had to walk past the fire and toss in a pinch of incense. This included not only high officials, eunuchs, scribes, servants, and slaves, but even Diocletian, Galerius, and their wives. After all, hadn't Jupiter saved their lives?

> One after another, all who lived and worked in the palace went up to the altar and dropped a pinch of incense on the flames. Only Dorotheus and Gorgogianus, two of Diocletian's most faithful secretaries who had been with him for years, refused to drop the incense on the altar. It was a poignant scene. Diocletian made an effort to persuade them, saying, "just one pinch will do." Dorotheus, speaking for his friend as well, gave a reply that was typical of a devout Christian in those days. "Domine," he said, "I have served you faithfully for many years. I would give my earthly life for you, but you are asking me to forfeit my eternal life. This I cannot do."[23]

Diocletian had no choice. These men defied the emperor publicly, and thus could not be forgiven. He had them tortured and beheaded.

Two weeks later, there was a second fire in the palace—one that started during a lightning storm, and was unlikely to have been caused by arson. Nevertheless, the blame was laid at the feet of the Christians, and the persecution sparked by the edict went on for years.

How many years?

Exactly 10.

"Do not fear any of those things which you are about to suffer," the prophecy had said. "Indeed, the devil is about to throw some of you into prison, that you may be tested, and you will have *tribulation ten days.* Be faithful until death, and I will give you the crown of life." (Revelation 2:10)

Remember: 10 days, in prophetic language, was 10 years (see Numbers 14:34; Ezekiel 4:6). Long before the Diocletian persecution began, the Christians knew it was coming. The God they worshipped, the humble carpenter's Son from Nazareth, was able to warn them centuries in advance that the church was going to experience some incredible hardship as they took the Gospel to the world.

The letter to Smyrna was a message from Someone who knew a thing or two about persecution, suffering, and death. He identifies Himself as "...the First and the Last, who was dead, and came to life." (Revelation 2:8) Why were the early Christians so willing to die for their faith? It was because the God whom they worshipped had already conquered the grave, and they knew that even if they died for their faith, death could not hold them forever.

Shortly before the persecution started, Jesus had also conquered the heart of a dejected divorcée named Helena. Her son had a front-row seat to the Diocletian persecutions. He was also the man who unwittingly fulfilled the prophecy, suddenly bringing the persecution to an end—exactly 10 years later.

FOOTNOTES FOR CHAPTER THREE

13. Foxe, John. *Foxe's Book of Martyrs*, Ch. 1, Sec. IX. Print.

14. Kousoulas, D. George. *The Life and Times of Constantine the Great*. Bethesda, MD: Rutledge, 2007. Print, 14.

15. Ibid., 16.

16. Jones, A. H. M. *Constantine and the Conversion of Europe*. Read Books Ltd., 2013. Digital, 17.

17. Lactantius. *The Complete Works of Lactantius: The Divine Institutes*. Digital, 14531-14535 on Kindle.

18. Kousoulas, D. George. *The Life and Times of Constantine the Great*. Bethesda, MD: Rutledge, 2007. Print, 95.

19. Eusebius. *Life of Constantine*. Heraklion Press. Digital, 1310-1312 on Kindle.

20. Ibid., 1316-1321.

21. Kousoulas, D. George. *The Life and Times of Constantine the Great*. Bethesda, MD: Rutledge, 2007. Print, 102.

22. Ibid.

23. Ibid., 107.

CHAPTER FOUR

THE ELEVATION OF CONSTANTIUS TO CAESAR was a disaster for Helena, but it proved to be advantageous for her son, Constantine. After his father's promotion, he was sent to live in Diocletian's palace. For 11 years, he worked directly for the emperor, during which time he watched Diocletian successfully squash the Manichean revolt in Egypt. He was also on hand in AD 303, when Diocletian issued his edict against the Christians.

Shortly after the 10-year persecution began, Diocletian did something no other emperor had ever done: he decided he was too old to rule, and so for the good of the empire, he chose to retire. He contacted Maximian in the west and suggested that both of them should step aside and promote their seconds-in-command to the top position. Of course, this meant that Diocletian would abdicate the throne while he was still at the top of his game, something you see a lot of in the 21st century. Back in 4th century Rome, it was unheard of.

Professor D. G. Kousoulas expressed it like this: "It was an idea that had virtually no precedent in Roman history. Tiberius had gone to the island of Capri and his sexual orgies but he had not really given up the purple, trying to govern from afar, with little success, to be sure. Nerva had retired after a few months, but Nerva was old and incompetent and had done the empire a favor by passing to Trajan the imperial mantle. Diocletian was neither Tiberius nor Nerva. His plan to step down was a deliberate and calculated move to preserve the tetrarchy and assure that the system would continue. Being, as ever, a prudent man, he realized that such a drastic step should be taken while he was in full control, with his personal authority undiminished."[24]

In September of AD 303, everybody went to the city of Rome for the great event. Rome hadn't really been the capital of the empire for a long time, but AD 303 was the 20th anniversary of Diocletian's reign, and the Eternal City seemed like the ideal place to hand over the reins of power to the two Caesars.

By the thousands, people poured into the streets to see the four rulers of the empire, something that they had never seen before. Rome might not have been the capital, but this event really underscored her position as the Mother City, the mother of the whole empire. (It was also the first time in 10 years that Constantine had seen his father. It was a reunion that happened just in time because, just a few years later, Flavius Constantius died. Later, on his deathbed, he asked his legions to promote his son to the position of Caesar, which would make him Constantine of the four tetrarchs. A humble peasant boy, born of a sordid one-night stand, was on his way to becoming one of the most powerful men in the world, testimony to the fact that the Roman Republic was a place of opportunity. In spite of a highly stratified social structure, anyone could, at least in theory, rise to the top.)

The festivities became rowdier as the days passed, and the festival-goers began to spiral out of control. What started as a 20-year anniversary and retirement party for Diocletian quickly became a long string of drunken parties and wild orgies. Lots of cheap wine flowed, people started singing bawdy songs and even had sexual relations in the street. The inhabitants of Rome were turning an event intended to be solemn and dignified into a drunken debauchery.

The behavior of the Romans disgusted Diocletian enough that he picked up and suddenly left town. He went north, to Ravenna, a city that would about 100 years later become the capital of the Western Roman Empire. During a cold and miserable winter in Ravenna, Diocletian suddenly got sick, possibly from the cold and wet weather on the 10-day trek from Rome. Galerius came to see him, and prompted him to renew his efforts against the Christian church. "Sir," he said, "those Christians are making trouble again."

We have no indication that his accusation was true, but Galerius' hatred of Christians was fierce. The restrictions that had been put on Christianity, he argued, were not enough. He suggested that the religion should be outlawed completely, the same way the Manicheans in Egypt had been outlawed a few years earlier.

In April of AD 304, Diocletian agreed to Galerius' demands. The persecution of the church was heightened, and merely *being* a Christian became a capital offense. *Foxe's Book of Martyrs* relates the stories of those who suffered:

> *Saturninus, a priest of Albitina, a town of Africa, after being tortured, was remanded to prison, and there starved to death. His four children, after being variously tormented, shared the same fate with their father.*

> *Dativas, a noble Roman senator; Thelico, a pious Christian.*

Victoria, a young lady of considerable family and fortune, with some others of less consideration, all auditors of Saturninus, were tortured in a similar manner, and perished by the same means.

Agrape, Chionia, and Irene, three sisters, were seized upon at Thessalonica, when Diocletian's persecution reached Greece. They were burnt, and received the crown of martyrdom in the flames, March 25, AD 304. The governor, finding that he could make no impression on Irene, ordered her to be exposed naked in the streets, which shameful order having been executed, a fire was kindled near the city wall, amidst whose flames her spirit ascended beyond the reach of man's cruelty.

Agatho, a man of a pious turn of mind, with Cassice, Philippa, and Eutychia, were martyred about the same time; but the particulars have not been transmitted to us.[25]

The list could go on. If Diocletian had paid attention to his former hesitation, he should have known what was going to happen: persecution would only strengthen the Christian church, and the believers would gladly go to their deaths. The centuries since Jesus had proven that biblical Christianity actually thrives under persecution. People whose God had sacrificed His own life on a cross didn't consider death to be a punishment. They considered dying for Christ to be a privilege.

Consider the words of Paul, who was also executed by the Romans: "For I am already being poured out as a drink offering, and the time of my departure is at hand. I have fought the good fight, I have finished the race, I have kept the faith. Finally, there is laid up for me the crown of righteousness, which the Lord, the righteous Judge, will give to me on that Day, and not to me only but also to all who have loved His appearing." (2 Timothy 4:6-8)

Not only had the book of Revelation predicted the 10-year persecution in Christ's message to Smyrna, but it had also painted a much larger picture of persecution in general, revealing that Roman hatred for Christ's followers was inspired by Satan:

> Now a great sign appeared in heaven: a woman clothed with the sun, with the moon under her feet, and on her head a garland of twelve stars. Then being with child, she cried out in labor and in pain to give birth.

> And another sign appeared in heaven: behold, a great, fiery red dragon having seven heads and ten horns, and seven diadems on his heads. His tail drew a third of the stars of heaven and threw them to the earth. And the dragon stood before the woman who was ready to give birth, to devour her Child as soon as it was born. She bore a male Child who was to rule all nations with a rod of iron. And her Child was caught up to God and His throne. Then the woman fled into the wilderness, where she has a place prepared by God, that they should feed her there one thousand two hundred and sixty days. (Revelation 12:1-6)

To John's 1st century audience, the language was obvious. The "woman" was a symbol for God's people, the church, who had been identified in other biblical passages as the bride of

Christ. In the Old Testament, the woman was Israel, the people of God who were waiting for the Child: Messiah. After Christ was born, the devil attempted to destroy Him, and ultimately failed. Jesus returned to heaven, so the dragon turned his wrath against the church instead:

> *Then I heard a loud voice saying in heaven, "Now salvation, and strength, and the kingdom of our God, and the power of His Christ have come, for the accuser of our brethren, who accused them before our God day and night, has been cast down. And they overcame him by the blood of the Lamb and by the word of their testimony, and they did not love their lives to the death. Therefore rejoice, O heavens, and you who dwell in them! Woe to the inhabitants of the earth and the sea! For the devil has come down to you, having great wrath, because he knows that he has a short time." Now when the dragon saw that he had been cast to the earth, he persecuted the woman who gave birth to the male Child. (Revelation 12:10-13)*

For those who had been paying attention to the prophecies, the persecution came as no big surprise. They were expecting it.

Occasionally, some of the less-committed believers buckled under pressure, betrayed the church and surrendered their Scriptures to the authorities. But as with every previous round of Roman persecution, the empire did nothing to stop the cause or halt the progress of Christianity.

Fortunately, the persecution of Christians did not prove to be universal in actual practice. The worst persecution took place in the eastern part of the empire, where Galerius was now rising to the position of Augustus. In the western regions, it wasn't quite as bad. In fact, some historians estimate that the best place to be a Christian during those years was Northern Europe.

Why was the persecution lighter in Northern Europe?

After Constantius divorced Helena to marry Theodora, he had a daughter named Anastasia. It's a Christian name, derived from the Greek word *anastasi,* which means "resurrection." Constantine's half-sister was named in honor of the resurrection of Christ.

That almost certainly means there were Christians in the house of Constantius. When he divorced Helena, Constantine reacted with the bitterness that children often suffer when parents divorce. Helena, on the other hand, turned to the religion of Jesus, which has always spoken powerfully to people experiencing disappointment. She was not turned out into the streets; she was still, to some extent, in the care of the Caesar.

We don't know with certainty that Helena's presence influenced the naming of Anastasia, but apparently someone sympathetic to Christianity must have convinced the Caesar to use the name. It also seems clear that the western Christians suffered less because of Christian influence in the palace.

It is also highly probable that Constantine had been exposed to Christianity before he left to live with Diocletian, which would help explain his later affinity for the faith.

At this point in the story, things start to get messy and complicated. As Diocletian and Maximian retired (and Diocletian was not in great health), Galerius decided that he would choose the new junior emperors. He picked Severus, a legion commander with a serious drinking problem, and his own nephew, Daia Maximus, a youth who was actually half-barbarian.

Daia was *really* bad news for the Christians.

Diocletian didn't like either of the two appointees.

"The men you have proposed to me," he said to Galerius, "are incapable, and you are asking me to entrust to them the empire?"

"I am in a position," answered Galerius, "to appreciate their merits."

Though we can't know Diocletian's mind at the time, he probably figured that, because he was retired, nobody would blame him if the empire fell apart. He did nothing to stop the appointments, and by not using the authority he still had, he unwittingly created a large problem in the West.

What happened?

Maximius, the now-retired Augustus of the West, whom Diocletian convinced to retire with him, had a son, Maxentius, who had just been completely passed over for the position of Caesar. (Of course, Constantine had also been passed over.)

Galerius must have realized the potential for hard feelings, because at this point, he forbade Constantine to leave the palace in Nicomedia. Why? He knew that if Constantine went west, where his father wanted him to be Caesar, there was going to be trouble.

Sure enough, Flavius Constantius asked for his son. Galerius couldn't deny the request of another Augustus, so he told Constantine he could leave, but not until the next day.

As Constantine waited to depart, Galerius tried to come up with an excuse to have the boy arrested. Constantine, suspicious of Galerius' motives, fled the palace, and on his way to Western

Europe, killed every horse along the imperial highway to stop
Galerius from pursuing him.

The historian Lactantius describes what ensued:

*Constantius, having become exceedingly ill, wrote to Galerius,
and requested that his son Constantine might be sent to see
him. He had made a like request long before, but in vain; for
Galerius meant nothing less than to grant it. On the contrary,
he laid repeated snares for the life of that young man, because
he durst not use open violence, lest he should stir up civil
wars against himself, and incur that which he most dreaded,
the hate and resentment of the army. Under pretence of
manly exercise and recreation, he made him combat with wild
beasts: but this device was frustrated; for the power of God
protected Constantine, and in the very moment of jeopardy
rescued him from the hands of Galerius. At length, Galerius,
when he could no longer avoid complying with the request
of Constantius, one evening gave Constantine a warrant to
depart, and commanded him to set out next morning with
the imperial dispatches. Galerius meant either to find some
pretext for detaining Constantine, or to forward orders to
Severus for arresting him on the road. Constantine discerned
his purpose; and therefore, after supper, when the emperor was
gone to rest, he hasted away, carried off from the principal
stages all the horses maintained at the public expense, and
escaped. Next day the emperor, having purposely remained in
his bed-chamber until noon, ordered Constantine to be called
into his presence; but he learnt that Constantine had set out
immediately after supper. Outrageous with passion, he ordered
horses to be made ready, that Constantine might be pursued*

and dragged back; and hearing that all the horses had been carried off from the great road, he could hardly refrain from tears. Meanwhile Constantine, journeying with incredible rapidity, reached his father, who was already about to expire. Constantius recommended his son to the soldiers, delivered the sovereign authority into his hands, and then died, as his wish had long been, in peace and quiet.[26]

Father and son were reunited in Gaul. Together, they went to war and defeated the Picts, a fierce pagan tribe from the British Isles. Constantine was so magnificent in battle that the men wanted him as their king, and they honored the request of his dying father. On July 25, AD 306, Constantine became ruler by popular acclamation. The men did not merely make him Caesar, the second in command; instead, they took his father's purple cape, and put it on Constantine's shoulders. They called him Augustus.

Galerius was not happy with this turn of events. History records that Constantine actually sent him a "gift"—a bust of himself. In a fit of rage, Galerius smashed it against the wall and threatened to have the messenger who brought it burned alive. His old mentor, Diocletian, talked him down from his fit of rage.

"I don't think you can fight this," Diocletian said, "so for the good of the empire, simply recognize Constantine as a *junior* emperor—recognize him as the Caesar."

It made sense, and Galerius followed his advice. He sent an imperial mantle to Constantine along with a friendly letter congratulating him as Caesar (not Augustus, but Caesar) of the West. And because Constantine was a patient man who was willing to bide his time, and because he was smart, he accepted the demotion graciously.

For the time being, the tetrarchy was restored: Galerius and Daia in the East, and Severus with Constantine in the West. But there one big problem: Maxentius, the son of retired western Augustus, Maximian, had been passed over. His title went to Constantine instead—and Roman politics being what it was, there was little he could do about it.

Then a golden opportunity suddenly presented itself. For years, the city of Rome had been exempt from paying taxes, because she was the "Mother of Cities." It was one of the few remaining privileges left to the residents of the city now that it was no longer the real center of the empire.

Galerius, however, decided to tax them. However fair his proposal might have been, it was a very unpopular move, and it presented an opportunity that Maxentius couldn't resist. He knew that over the centuries, the Roman Senate had slowly been stripped of its power. In the distant past, the Senate had actually chosen emperors, but now it was usually the army that did it. Diocletian had come to power by the acclamation of the army, and the same thing had happened with Constantine. The old patricians of the Senate were virtually powerless; the glory days of the Roman Senate were long gone.

The new tax underscored it.

Maxentius, smelling an opportunity, traveled to Rome and told the Senate they could revive their own power, prestige, and glory. "Declare me the emperor," he said, "and I will restore Rome's glory."

It was too good to resist—but the Senate feared that Maxentius was too young and inexperienced to take the reins of power. "No problem," Maxentius told them, "I'll be happy to serve as an assistant emperor. My father is willing to come out of retirement; make him the senior ruler instead. If he is emperor, I will assist him."

It was a lie. Maxentius had no intention of involving his father. The Senate believed him, however, and jumped on the idea. His father did come to Rome for a short while, but after a series of political maneuvers, Maxentius made himself the emperor in Rome, theoretically adding a *fifth* ruler to the tetrarchy.

It didn't take long before the Senate's initial fears about Maxentius were realized. He was not fit to rule. His power went to his head, and he began to fancy himself the ruler of the whole world. He began to party, sleep around, and sell favors to his favorite men. He quickly lost everyone's respect.

In the meantime, the Christian influence in Constantine's household began to grow. When Maximian (the old Augustus, and father to Maxentius) died, Constantine buried him in a coffin—a Christian custom. His stepmother Theodora also quietly converted, and kept a Christian minister right on the premises. Now both his mother and stepmother were followers of the Nazarene, and of course, his stepsister was named for the resurrection.

There was a great deal of Christian influence in the home of Constantine. Constantine himself, however, continued as a pagan, a sun worshipper who sacrificed to Apollo before every significant battle.

And now a battle was brewing against Maxentius, whose claim to power could not be permitted. Constantine was determined to do something about his claim to the throne in Rome. Already, both Severus and Galerius had been unsuccessful in trying to oust Maxentius. Severus, for his trouble, ended up slain; Galerius, having failed, kept his reign but was more or less neutered and no longer a threat.

In AD 311, Galerius died a terrible death, described (if not with a bit of exaggeration) by the historian Lactantius like this:

And now, when Galerius was in the eighteenth year of his reign, God struck him with an incurable plague. A malignant ulcer formed itself low down in his secret parts, and spread by degrees. The physicians attempted to eradicate it, and healed up the place affected. But the sore, after having been skinned over, broke out again; a vein burst, and the blood flowed in such quantity as to endanger his life. The blood, however, was stopped, although with difficulty. The physicians had to undertake their operations anew, and at length they cicatrized the wound. In consequence of some slight motion of his body, Galerius received a hurt, and the blood streamed more abundantly than before. He grew emaciated, pallid, and feeble, and the bleeding then stanched. The ulcer began to be insensible to the remedies applied, and a gangrene seized all the neighboring parts. It diffused itself the wider the more the corrupted flesh was cut away, and everything employed as the means of cure served but to aggravate the disease. The masters of the healing art withdrew. Then famous physicians were brought in from all quarters; but no human means had any success. Apollo and Æsculapius were besought importunately for remedies: Apollo did prescribe, and the distemper augmented. Already approaching to its deadly crisis, it had occupied the lower regions of his body: his bowels came out, and his whole seat putrefied. The luckless physicians, although without hope of overcoming the malady, ceased not to apply fomentations and administer medicines. The humours having been repelled, the distemper attacked his intestines, and worms were generated in his body. The stench was so foul as to pervade not only the pal-

ace, but even the whole city; and no wonder, for by that time the
passages from his bladder and bowels, having been devoured by
the worms, became indiscriminate, and his body, with intolerable
anguish, was dissolved into one mass of corruption.[27]

Severus and Galerius had failed. Could Constantine succeed?

Constantine began his long march, fighting his way toward the Eternal City. The Caesar was not just a great leader; he was also a fighter. During battles, he didn't command from the rear but joined his men on the field, an act that inspired his troops to the point where they were unstoppable.

Inside the city walls of Rome, people were starting to get nervous. They knew that Constantine was coming. To put their minds at ease, Maxentius did the same thing Nebuchadnezzar's grandson Belshazzar did on the eve of the Persian sack of Babylon: he threw a party. It was a move designed to pacify the masses. If the king feels like celebrating with a party, then how bad could the situation be?

Maxentius probably should have learned from history. After all, things didn't end so well for Belshazzar that night: "That very night Belshazzar, king of the Chaldeans, was slain." (Daniel 5:30)

On the 26th of October, AD 312, the festivities in the city of Rome were really gearing up. Maxentius was celebrating five years on his throne, and he was determined to make everyone understand that he could never fall. The citizens of Rome began to feel better, because if Maxentius was willing to party, then he must feel confident. Maybe the city walls would be enough to stop Constantine, after all.

In fact, Maxentius was counting on the city walls to protect him, not because Constantine couldn't defeat them, but because he knew that Constantine's men would be hesitant to attack the Mother City. It had been tried by other Roman armies in the past who lost their courage, because attacking Rome felt like attacking your mother. If Maxentius had to leave the city to face Constantine, he would likely lose; if he could stay inside, he had a distinct psychological advantage.

Nobody wanted a battle inside the city. Even those who supported Maxentius (there were fewer of those by the day) wanted the fight to be over quickly, out in the fields, away from town. Maxentius was determined not to let that happen.

So that October, the people inside the city celebrated Maxentius' reign. They went to the chariot races in the old Circus Maximus. Then, immediately after the first race, a voice suddenly shouted from the stands: "Hey! Maxentius! Are you afraid to fight Constantine out in the open?" Another voice shouted out from another section of the stands: "Are you a coward hiding behind the city walls?" More and more voices, in unison, shouted the taunts: "Are you a coward?"

We don't know who started the taunting, but it was probably a plant, one of Constantine's men who had quietly slipped into the games as an instigator. If so, the tactic was very effective. A lot of people didn't like Maxentius, and before long, most the crowd was mocking him as a coward. If Constantine had, indeed, orchestrated the whole thing, it was a brilliant tactical move, because *he* didn't really want to fight inside the city, either. He knew the advantage was his on the outside.

Maxentius was furious. Minutes before, the same mob was cheering him and hailing him; now he was the subject of their open derision. He stormed out of the arena and went to the Senate. He ordered them to consult an ancient set of books known as the *Sibylline Books* (not to be confused with the *Sibylline Oracles*), and he asked them: "Is there a prophecy in there? Is there something to indicate who would win in a battle with Constantine?"

The next morning, the Senate came back with an answer: "Tomorrow, the enemy of Rome will perish." Maxentius was delighted, because he assumed the enemy of Rome was none other than Constantine.

There was just one problem: if the enemy of Rome was to die tomorrow, then there had to be a battle the next day. Constantine's army was camping safely at Saxa Rubra, nine miles from the city. If Maxentius didn't attack him, there could be no fulfillment of the prophecy. He would have to strike first.

Outside the city, someone gave Constantine the bad news: Maxentius had discovered a prophecy that predicted his victory. The *Sibylline Books* had predicted that Constantine would be killed. It was a devastating psychological blow to his troops. The Romans were superstitious, and a prophecy against them from the *Sibylline Books* was no laughing matter. They had started the day nervous about attacking the Mother City, and now they were becoming distraught.

Constantine saw that their spirits were beginning to fall. He knew that *he* needed an omen to counter the one that Maxentius had devised—something to bolster his army's courage.

That's when one of the most famous episodes in world history suddenly unfolded.

Constantine came up with his own talisman: the *chi-rho,* a symbol he ordered his men to paint on their shields. The *chi-rho* is really two Greek letters blended together: the letter *chi,* which looks like our letter X (but is really a CH), and the letter *rho,* which looks like our letter P (but is really the letter R). Today, it is widely recognized as a Christian symbol, because together, the two letters create the first letters in the word *Christ:* CHR.

The symbol predates Christianity, however. Modern Christians tend to see it as a cross, but it was actually developed by pagans. The letters CHR also formed the first letters in the word *Chrestus,* which means "good luck." This is likely how Constantine used it.

He told his men that he had received a message from the gods in a dream. "I saw this symbol, and I want all of you to paint it on your shields. It's a guarantee that we will win."

It was exactly what he needed.

There's a long-standing legend in regard to this story. Many accounts say that Constantine didn't have a dream; he actually had a *vision,* where he saw the *chi-rho* superimposed on the sun. Most versions now say that that he saw a *cross* superimposed on the sun, and he heard a voice saying (in Latin), "*In hoc signo vinces*"—"Conquer in this sign." In other words, Constantine was instructed by a heavenly messenger to conquer in the sign of the Christian cross, by the power of Jesus Christ.

The historian Eusebius tells the story like this:

> *He said that about noon, when the day was already beginning to decline, he saw with his own eyes the trophy of a cross of light in the heavens, above the sun, and bearing the inscription, Conquer by this. At this sight he himself was struck with amazement, and his whole army also, which followed him on this expedition, and witnessed the miracle.*[28]

Christians love to tell Eusebius' version of the story, which states that Constantine was told by a heavenly messenger to conquer by the power of Jesus Christ.

There's just one problem with the story: it's probably a legend. Shortly after Constantine's stunning victory, the Senate erected a magnificent arch to commemorate it. It still stands next to the Colosseum in Rome, and it recounts the story of his conquest. If the story of the vision were true, it would be so pivotal that you would expect to find some mention of it in the official telling—but it's not there. Search the Arch of Constantine from top to bottom, and you will find no mention of Christ or Christianity. There is no cross, and no mention of *In hoc signo vinces*.

There *is* an inscription, which translated, reads like this:

> *To the Emperor Caesar Flavius Constantine, the Greatest, Pius, Felix, Augustus: inspired by (a) divinity, in the greatness of his mind, he used his army to save the state by the just force of arms from a tyrant on the one hand and every kind of factionalism on the other; therefore the Senate and the People of Rome have dedicated this exceptional arch to his triumphs.*

The only possible reference that you can find to Christianity is a vague reference to the inspiration of a "divinity." Which divinity was that? It does not say. Again, there is no mention of Jesus or a cross superimposed on the sun.

There is no mention of the vision for another decade, when Constantine suddenly mentions it to Eusebius, likely in an attempt to persuade the Christians of his divine calling.

It wasn't a cross that Constantine's men painted on their shields—it was a *chi-rho*, a pagan good luck charm their leader had claimed to see in a dream. It was enough, however, to rally the troops. Now they, too, had an omen—a sign that the gods who had aided Rome throughout her history would favor their attempt to liberate the city from Maxentius.

What happened next was, literally, history in the making: the famous Battle of the Milvian Bridge.

Maxentius' general, a man named Rufius Volusianus, hatched a plan. On October 28, AD 312, early in the morning, a strong force with the Praetorian Guards at the front crossed the Tiber River over the Milvian Bridge and another pontoon bridge erected nearby. Another group of soldiers, crossing over other bridges downstream, would join the fray and help wipe out Constantine's army once and for all. (The Milvian Bridge still exists today, a place where lovers go to place padlocks as a sign of their everlasting love for each other.)

Volusianus counted on two things. First, the element of surprise (he assumed that Constantine would not expect Maxentius' troops to leave the protection of the city and its walls), always a crucial factor in battle. Second, he figured that if he attacked early in the morning, the men would be half-asleep and thus even more vulnerable to the assault.

The plan was to attack, strike a devastating blow, and then quickly retreat to safety on the other side of the river. Get in, hit hard, get out—a fairly common military maneuver.

Maxentius' general believed that Constantine's men would come after them. When they did, Volusianus would use the pontoon bridge as a trap. As soon as Constantine's troops followed him over, he would break the bridge in half, trapping Constantine's men on the north bank of the river. (Roman engineers had rigged it so that it would collapse.) That would make Constantine's men sitting ducks, out in the open, and Maxentius' archers would rain down a shower of arrows on them, killing them all.

If the Sibylline prophecy was correct, it would be a success. Constantine would die, and the threat to Maxentius' reign would be over.

It was a good plan, but, as the old saying goes, "The best-laid plans of mice and men often go awry," which is exactly what happened. Constantine and his army responded to the surprise attack much faster than anybody could have anticipated; there was no time to retreat over the bridge. Instead, Constantine caught up with Maxentius' men before *they* could cross the bridge, and started plowing into them with incredible ferocity.

General Volusianus learned the hard way what Helmuth von Moltke, a 19th century head of the Prussian army, famously observed: "No battle plan ever survives first contact with the enemy."

With the Praetorian Guards fighting on the front lines, Maxentius' horsemen and foot soldiers clashed with Constantine's troops. Hundreds were killed or injured on both sides of this savage battle.

The sun was already over the mountain ridges to the east when Maxentius rode out of Rome to join his troops, certain that by then they would have put Constantine's troops to flight. Instead, he saw that the battle was raging and that his men were being pushed back toward the river. The air was thick with the clanging of swords, the cries of wounded men, the curses of warriors fighting for their lives, the neighing of frightened horses, and the smell of blood mixing with the smell of sweat. Maxentius' appearance must have lifted momentarily the fighting spirit of his soldiers but Constantine's men kept pushing the enemy relentlessly toward the river, stepping over the bodies of the men already dead or dying, forcing many to jump into the river where many drowned as they were pulled down by the weight of their uniforms.[29]

As Constantine saw the enemy pull back, he ordered a full assault, leading the way himself. He was on his horse, with his sword raised high in the air, no doubt inspiring the troops to follow his lead.

This attack, with Constantine at the head, created a panic among Maxentius' troops, and when Maxentius saw that the battle had turned against him, he quickly ordered his men to retreat back over the Milvian Bridge and into the city. They stampeded for the bridge, which was far too narrow for hundreds of panicked men at once—most of them loaded down with armor and equipment. The men started to push and shove, and the panic got worse by the minute.

That's when Maxentius made a fatal mistake: he rode out into the middle of the Milvian Bridge, hoping to get control over the scene. However, in the stampede and panic, the emperor himself got pushed off his horse and fell into the waters of the Tiber River. His armor dragged him under the surface, as it did to so many other soldiers. His mud-covered body was found lying in the reeds the next morning.

The battle raged that day, not ending until mid-afternoon, with great losses on both sides, with Maxentius' troops suffering the worst, even though they had outnumbered Constantine's men significantly. Thousands were wounded, and hundreds drowned in the Tiber River. Many others, seeing that all was lost, threw down their weapons and gave up. Others managed to get back to the city, where they told the stunned inhabitants what had happened: Maxentius was dead, his army had been crushed, and Constantine was the victor.

The next morning, on October 29, Constantine rode triumphantly into the city of Rome, and again, his soldiers painted a *chi-rho* on their shields—now most certainly a symbol of good luck.

His grand entry was unlike any the citizens of Rome had ever seen. Usually, when a victor rode into town, he led a procession of captives and he showed off the spoils of war. But this time, Constantine entered the city empty-handed, with one notable exception: he did have the head of Maxentius on a spear.

News of the emperor's demise spread rapidly in Rome, but there apparently were also concerns that it was a false report. It was felicitous for the victorious side in these circumstances that Maxentius' body was recovered. Constantine knew how to take advantage of the symbolic capital that the Tiber had washed ashore. As he made ready his triumphal entrance into the city the next day, the body was hacked in pieces and the head of the drowned emperor severed from the torso and affixed to a spear. It led the victor's procession as an imposing sign of his total victory.

A few months later in faraway Trier, when Constantine had left Italy again and returned to his main residence on the Moselle, a panegyrist recalled this event. The orator reports that "after the body had been found and hacked up, the entire populace of Rome broke out in vengeful rejoicing, and throughout the whole City where it was carried affixed to a spear that sinful head did not cease to suffer disfiguration, and meanwhile, in the customary guests of a triumph, it was mocked by insulting its bearer, since he suffered the deserts of another's head." Even though severed heads had now and then acquired a certain indecorous significance in Roman civil wars, on October 29, 312, for the first time in Roman history, the head of a toppled emperor was paraded through the city in a triumph to the jubilation of the masses. It was the head of an emperor who had ruled Rome for six years and despite sporadic conflict with his subjects over that time had built up an extensive network of supporters, clients, and other beneficiaries at all levels of society.

The sight of this emperor's head affixed to the end of a spear as it was carried around the city, exposed to insult and outrage, must have moved observers even more profoundly, because Maxentius was still an emperor who enjoyed considerable dynastic prestige—even though he had not been recognized by the regular Tetrarchs: he was none other than the biological son of the emperor Maximian (who had been consecrated in Rome not long before) and thus in formal terms ranked significantly higher than Constantine.[30]

There was one other key difference between this parade and many other triumphal entries like it—a difference that should not be overlooked. The parade made its way to the Capitoline Hill, where conquering heroes always offered sacrifices at the Temple of Jupiter. But this time, there was no sacrifice, because Constantine didn't give Jupiter the credit. This time, the honor went to the Christian God. While the story of the cross superimposed on the sun is likely mere legend, Constantine *was* profoundly influenced by his mother's religion. From that moment on, nothing in the Western world would ever be the same.

FOOTNOTES FOR CHAPTER FOUR

24. Kousoulas, D. George. *The Life and Times of Constantine the Great*. Bethesda, MD: Rutledge, 2007. Print, 120.

25. Foxe, John. *Foxe's Book of Martyrs*, Ch. 2. Print.

26. Lactantius. *The Complete Works of Lactantius: The Divine Institutes*. Digital, 14865-14877 on Kindle.

27. Ibid., 15062-15080.

28. Eusebius. *Life of Constantine, Book I*, Ch. 28. Heraklion Press. Digital.

29. Kousoulas, D. George. *The Life and Times of Constantine the Great*. Bethesda, MD: Rutledge, 2007. Print, 247.

30. Wienand, Johannes. *Contested Monarchy: Integrating the Roman Empire in the Fourth Century AD*. Oxford University Press, 2015. Print, 177-178.

CHAPTER FIVE

At times, historians speculate about the past by writing alternate histories that explore what might have been if things had turned out differently.

In 1962, for example, writer Philip K. Dick published an alternate history of World War II in his award-winning novel, *The Man in the High Castle.* His version of events has the war concluding in 1947—with a victory by the Axis powers. It is the story of Americans living under totalitarian rule, with Japan and Germany dividing the United States: Japan ruling the West Coast, Germany ruling the East. It was inspired by another novel published a decade earlier, *Bring the Jubilee,* an alternative history of the American Civil War that contemplates what might have happened if the Confederacy had won.

Such histories raise a good question: what would life be like today had things in history turned out differently? What would have happened if, perchance, the southern states had actually won? How different would our world today be had a young Austrian art student by the name of Adolph Hitler been accepted to art school instead of being rejected? Had he gotten into school, Hitler might have gone on a completely different trajectory than the one that led him to become the head of the Nazi party. There might not have been a Second World War. Or what would have happened had President John F. Kennedy, heeding the advice of his security, not traveled in a convertible through the streets of Dallas? Suppose, during the Cuban Missile Crisis, the Soviets and the Americans actually *did* launch nuclear weapons. How would that have changed history?

If Constantine had lost at the Battle of the Milvian Bridge, it would have changed everything. You and I would be living in a radically different world.

Why?

Constantine pulled Christianity out of the shadows and made it the premier religion of the Roman Empire. Influenced heavily by his mother's religion, he suspected that the Christian God had been responsible for his victory. Unfortunately, he began to think of Jesus as the new Roman "God of War," a dramatic departure from the actual teachings of Christ. Jesus had stated, "My kingdom is not of this world. If My kingdom were of this world, My servants would fight, so that I should not be delivered to the Jews; but now My kingdom is not from here." (John 18:36)

Constantine looked to the Christian religion as the new unifying element that would restore lasting peace and stability to the empire. He admired the tenacity of the Christians, who had managed to survive the worst that Rome could throw at them. To his way of thinking, Christians were in perfect solidarity and provided an enviable model of unity. If he could import their attitude into the rest of the empire, he could secure it permanently.

Shortly after defeating Maxentius, Constantine entered Rome. He proved himself remarkably generous and magnanimous to his former enemies. Instead of executing General Volusianus, he appointed him to important posts in the city, a move so unusual that it has caused some historians to suspect that Volusianus may have been working for Constantine all along. Furthermore, instead of punishing the Senate for their role in enabling Maxentius, he promised to restore them to their former power and glory. The senators were so thankful to Constantine that they commissioned the Arch of Constantine, a magnificent monument that stands to this day.

The Arch of Constantine is not his most enduring legacy, however. The day Constantine rode into the city—the day he refused to offer sacrifice at the Temple of Jupiter on the Capitoline Hill—was the day that the paths of Constantine and Jesus finally met. What happened next was so explosive, so consequential, that it changed the face of the empire, it changed the face of world politics, and it changed the very nature of the Christian church.

Under Constantine, the religion of Jesus took on a new flavor, because the Prince of Peace had become the Roman God of War. In a single moment, Jesus moved from being the God of the underdog to the God of the emperor. In a manner of speaking, Jesus was made to say, "Blessed is the general who sacks the city of Rome."

There's just no way to underestimate how important this moment was. In a sense, and without any exaggeration, we could say that we still live in the shadow of Constantine's empire. Just a few weeks after Constantine's win, the *chi-rho* started showing up all over the city. It was now Constantine's symbol, and as a result, it came to be identified with Christianity.

Many things that were distinctly Roman suddenly became Christian. For example, when you hear the word "basilica," most people typically think of a Christian church, and rightly so, because for the last 1,700 years, that's the way the word has been used.

Today, a basilica is a church that has been granted special ceremonial rights or privileges by the Bishop of Rome, otherwise known as the Pope. But originally, a basilica was not a Christian building; in fact, it wasn't even a religious building. A basilica was a public courthouse, like the famous one used by Maxentius and then by Constantine after the Battle of the Milvian Bridge. A significant portion of the Basilica of Maxentius still stands to this day, right next to the Arch of Constantine. After Maxentius, Constantine continued to use it. It was the place where he did his official business.

Just a few blocks away is another notable basilica, one of the most famous in the world: the Basilica of St. John Lateran. Structurally, the two basilicas are stunningly similar—identical in some aspects—and that's because after Constantine, the church inherited its architecture from the Roman Empire. The Christians were no longer a fringe group, an outside religion forced to exist in *spite* of the empire. On the contrary, they were now the heart of the empire itself, suddenly blessed with the favor of the emperor. They were given the keys to the halls of power.

Diocletian had attempted to unify the empire with a tetrarchy; Constantine had other plans. In the years immediately following the defeat of Maxentius, Constantine went on to conquer the rest of the empire and become its sole ruler. The tetrarchy was dead. The illegitimate child of a one-night stand had made it to the very top.

But now, with all rivals gone, Constantine knew that he was going to have to find some other way to keep the vast empire together—some way to achieve harmony among so immense and disparate a domain.

Enter Christianity. Here's where he saw value in the Christian religion. For Constantine, Christians looked as if they were so perfectly united, so perfectly in agreement, that nothing could make them fall. Having been close at hand for the Diocletian persecutions, he must have seen how in so many cases, these Christians were willing to die rather than offer a pinch of incense.

He hoped to tap into their resolve. If he could use their religion to create a people as dedicated to the nation as they were to Christ, it would seal and secure his authority.

Constantine himself, however, had not become a Christian. Not really. Tradition says that he underwent a radical conversion the day before the Battle of the Milvian Bridge, a story he was pleased to tell a decade later to a delighted crowd assembled to celebrate his reign. But if Constantine had *truly* become a Christian that day, he was remarkably silent about it. There was no word of a vision, and no word of a conversion the day he marched into the city. The Senate failed to mention such things in *their* telling of the story.

There is no mention of it for *10 years*.

· There is much reason to doubt the conversion of Constantine. Long after his supposed epiphany, he continued killing off relatives he considered to be political threats, including his own wife and son—hardly the actions of a sincere devotee to the Prince of Peace.

Around AD 305, Constantine had a firstborn son, named Flavius Julius Crispus. It is uncertain whether Crispus' mother, Minervina, was ever Constantine's legal wife, for not much is known about her. But he did marry a woman named Fausta in AD 307, and she would bear him three other sons.

Constantine had groomed his firstborn, Crispus, very well, and when Crispus grew up, he made his father proud by fighting successfully against the Alamanni and Franks in AD 320. Then in another war, Crispus made an important contribution to his father's triumph with a brilliant naval victory.

To this day, no one knows the reason why, but Constantine had Crispus executed in AD 326, when the boy was only 21 years old. Why would he have done that?

Zosimus, a pagan who didn't like Constantine's embrace of Christianity, wrote the following:

> When he came to Rome, he was filled with pride and arrogance. He decided to begin his impious acts at home, for he put to death his son Crispus, on suspicion of debauching his stepmother Fausta without any regard to the ties of nature. And when his own mother Helena expressed deep sorrow for this atrocity, lamenting with great bitterness the death of the young man, Constantine, pretending to comfort her, applied a remedy worse than the disease. He ordered a bath to be heated to an extremely high temperature, had Fausta thrown in, and a short time later she was taken out dead.[31]

Though much is shrouded in mystery, some truth might have existed in the story of Crispus having sexual relations with his stepmother, Fausta. Some speculate that she might have purposely seduced him, and then ratted him out, in hopes of getting him in trouble with his father. If she did, it worked.

Why would she do it? Perhaps, knowing that the aging Constantine would need an heir, she was trying to get the most obvious rival, Crispus, out of the way, opening a path to the throne for one of her own sons. Whatever the reason, Crispus was put to death and then, not much later, so was Fausta, and in an incredibly horrific manner. Some speculate that perhaps Constantine, finding out that she did seduce the young man, for the reasons stated above, got so angry that he was purposefully cruel.

Still, Constantine's actions were hardly those of a born-again Christian. In the words of Jesus, "Therefore by their fruits ye shall know them." (Matthew 7:20) It's not that godly people don't make mistakes. King David himself seduced a soldier's wife and then, when she became pregnant, had her husband killed to cover his tracks. Good people sometimes do bad things. But in the case of David, we have a record of his considerable regret and repentance. To the best of his ability, he made things right.

There is no record of Constantine admitting wrongdoing or regretting his actions. He continued to act like a pagan long after his supposed conversion—and he put off his own baptism until he was practically on his deathbed.

There are enough holes in the story to justify a healthy skepticism about Constantine's conversion. What seems more likely is that Constantine embellished his story over time, and the *chi-rho* symbol he painted on his men's shields slowly morphed into the vision-in-the-sky and voice-from-heaven tale over the span of the following 10 years.

There was no question Constantine *knew* about the Christian God, because he had believers in his family: his mother, his stepmother, and other members of his household were also probably converts. It's likely true that he credited the Christian God for his victory. He had a healthy respect for the faith, coupled with admiration for the dedication of Christ's followers.

But *respecting* God and submitting your life and will to Him are two different things. Constantine believed that if he painted his empire with the veneer of Christianity, then the people who were willing to die for Jesus would be willing to die for him. He believed that if he could merge the Christian church with Rome, then the Christians would prove eternally loyal to the empire.

Under pagan emperors, religion and state had been united; under Constantine, the state would be wed to the Christian church.

One of the first things he did, after living in the Lateran Palace for a few weeks, was to give it as a gift to Miltiades, the Bishop of Rome. Up to that point, the Bishop of Rome had essentially lived in poverty on the other side of the Tiber River. He was now the master of an impressive palace. It was not the Lateran Palace which is now attached to the Basilica of St. John Lateran. The original was badly damaged in two fires during the 1300s, after which the Bishop of Rome eventually moved to his present home in the Vatican. What was left of the original was demolished in the late 1500s, and the present structure was built to replace it.

Today, the Lateran Palace continues to be a significant Christian building. It is currently home to the Vicar General of Rome, an official representative of the Pope. The Bishop of Rome is responsible for the world; the Vicar General assumes his responsibilities for the city itself.

But the only reason the Lateran Palace is a Christian building at all is because Constantine gave it to the church.

This move was a clear and unambiguous signal about the direction in which the new emperor of Rome was leading the empire. The city's pagan population began to eye him with suspicion: Constantine had refused to thank Jupiter for his victory, and now he had given the Christian bishop one of the most prestigious pieces of real estate in the city. Then, to top it all off, he built a massive basilica, the original St. Peter's, on the Vaticanus mountain. It was not the St. Peter's that stands in the same location today. The present basilica is actually a replacement that was built on the original site in the 1500s, about the time that the Protestant Reformation was sweeping across Europe. Constantine had built a slightly smaller version, and if you climb down under the present St. Peter's, you can still see parts of Constantine's original building.

Thanks to Constantine, Christianity had come to Rome for good. In the western half of the empire, persecution came to a grinding halt. In the east, however, persecution continued under Emperor Licinius (Constantine had not yet eliminated all of his rivals). The next year, in AD 313, Constantine traveled to the city of Milan to attend an important state wedding, and while there, he met with Licinius and convinced him to stop persecuting. Together, they issued the Edict of Milan, a document that completely reversed Diocletian's original edict, formally ending persecution and granting full religious liberty to the Christians:

> When I, Constantine Augustus, as well as I, Licinius Augustus, fortunately met near Mediolanurn (Milan), and were considering everything that pertained to the public welfare and security, we thought, among other things which we saw would be for the good of many, those regulations pertaining to the reverence of the Divinity ought certainly to be made first, so that we might grant to the Christians and others

full authority to observe that religion which each preferred; whence any Divinity whatsoever in the seat of the heavens may be propitious and kindly disposed to us and all who are placed under our rule. And thus by this wholesome counsel and most upright provision we thought to arrange that no one whatsoever should be denied the opportunity to give his heart to the observance of the Christian religion, of that religion which he should think best for himself, so that the Supreme Deity, to whose worship we freely yield our hearts, may show in all things His usual favor and benevolence. Therefore, your Worship should know that it has pleased us to remove all conditions whatsoever, which were in the rescripts formerly given to you officially, concerning the Christians and now any one of these who wishes to observe Christian religion may do so freely and openly, without molestation. We thought it fit to commend these things most fully to your care that you may know that we have given to those Christians free and unrestricted opportunity of religious worship. When you see that this has been granted to them by us, your Worship will know that we have also conceded to other religions the right of open and free observance of their worship for the sake of the peace of our times, that each one may have the free opportunity to worship as he pleases; this regulation is made that we may not seem to detract from any dignity or any religion.

Moreover, in the case of the Christians especially we esteemed it best to order that if it happens anyone heretofore has bought from our treasury from anyone whatsoever, those places where they were previously accustomed to assemble, concerning which a certain decree had been made and a letter sent to you officially, the same shall be restored to the Christians without payment or any claim of recompense and without any kind of fraud or deception. Those, moreover, who have obtained the same by gift, are likewise to return them at once to the Christians. Besides, both those who have purchased and those who have secured them by gift, are to appeal to the vicar if they seek any recompense from our bounty, that they may be cared for through our clemency. All this property ought to be delivered at once to the community of the Christians through your intercession, and without delay. And since these Christians are known to have possessed not only those places in which they were accustomed to assemble, but also other property, namely the churches, belonging to them as a corporation and not as individuals, all these things which we have included under the above law, you will order to be restored, without any hesitation or controversy at all, to these Christians, that is to say to the corporations and their conventicles: providing, of course, that the above arrangements be followed so that those who return the same without payment, as we have said, may hope for an indemnity from our bounty. In all these circumstances you ought to tender your most efficacious intervention to the community of the Christians, that our command may be carried into effect as quickly as possible, whereby, moreover, through our clemency, public order may be secured. Let this be done so that, as we have said above, Divine favor towards us, which, under the most important circumstances we have already experienced, may, for all time, preserve and prosper our successes together with the good of the state. Moreover, in order that the statement of this decree of our good will may come to the notice of all, this rescript, published by your decree, shall be announced everywhere and brought to the knowledge of all, so that the decree of this, our benevolence, cannot be concealed.[32]

A number of important provisions were found in the edit. The Christians were to be free to worship according to the dictates of conscience. The property that had been confiscated from them during the 10-year reign of terror was to be returned, and if someone found themselves in possession of such property, they could appeal to Constantine's government for compensation.

The church was no longer a fringe group, but now a legitimate corporation, a part of the Roman Empire.

You will notice, however, that the number-one concern was still the unity of the Roman Empire: "…whence any Divinity whatsoever in the seat of the heavens may be propitious and kindly disposed to us and all who are placed under our rule." Constantine was motivated by politics, but nonetheless, the edict was a major leap forward for Christians, who for years had been scorned, hated, and at times severely persecuted. Now they were the darlings of the emperor.

Constantine had unwittingly fulfilled the prophecy of Revelation's letter to Smyrna, bringing the Diocletian persecution to a close precisely 10 years after it began. The 10 days of suffering were finished:

> *Do not fear any of those things which you are about to suffer. Indeed, the devil is about to throw some of you into prison, that you may be tested, and you will have tribulation ten days. Be faithful until death, and I will give you the crown of life. (Revelation 2:10)*

Ten years, exactly as predicted in the Word of God.

It would be reasonable to think that, with the Edict of Milan, the story was over. Christianity was no longer a hated sect, and with the emperor's protection, nobody could touch them, and they all lived happily ever after.

But it wasn't so simple. The Edict of Milan didn't establish Christianity as the official religion of the empire, not in the way that, for instance, Anglicanism is the official religion of England. But it did establish Christians as the reason for granting full religious liberty. And there was no question that Christians had suddenly moved from underdog to a position of privilege—a position they would hold for many centuries to come.

The sudden change in fortune, however, also changed the face of Christianity. One could argue, and justly so, that the change was ultimately not for the better.

Christianity, however, was nowhere near as unified as Constantine had originally thought. Within months of his victory, Constantine made an unsettling discovery—one that, unfortunately, many people still discover when they get to know the Christian community today: Christians can be anything *but* united. On the basic essentials (God exists, Jesus is God's Son, Christ died on the cross) widespread agreement exists. But on many other doctrines and the finer nuances of the faith, the divisions can be deep. There is a reason that modern Christianity has fragmented into tens of thousands of unique church bodies. Christians are still merely human, which means that they are imperfect sinners in desperate need of a perfect God. Christians know how to argue, just like everybody else. (The Jews sometimes joke among themselves: "Two Jews, three opinions." One could argue that Christians aren't much different.)

In the face of Constantine's hope for a unified Christian empire, a controversy erupted on the other side of the Mediterranean, in Egypt. During the Diocletian persecution, a lot of Christian leaders had caved in under pressure. When the Romans came to confiscate Christian books, they turned in their Bibles, and many of them even left the church, pretending to have forsaken the faith. When the persecution suddenly ended, and it was safe—even easy—to be a Christian, they suddenly wanted to be back in the church.

That ruffled the feathers of those who had *not* wavered. Those who stayed the course—those who remained true to the faith during those dark days when, indeed, the words of Paul ("Yea, and all that would live godly in Christ Jesus shall suffer persecution." [2 Timothy 3:12]) were being fulfilled in a powerful way—wouldn't hear of it.

They called those who had abandoned the church *traditores* (it's where we get the word "traitor"), and they didn't think that those people should be readmitted to the church. If they *did* return, they certainly couldn't hold church office. If you had been baptized by a *traditore* before they had bolted in the face of persecution, your baptism was considered null and void and you would have to do it again.

The people who wanted to keep the traitors out of the church had a leader by the name of Donatus Magnus; thus, they were called the "Donatists," and their struggle has become known in church history as the "Donatist Controversy." The Donatists had wanted Donatus to become the Bishop of Carthage, in North Africa. However, Carthage already had a bishop, Caecilian, who favored bringing the traitors back in.

It wasn't a minor squabble. It threatened to tear apart the church in North Africa, something that Constantine didn't want. When it became apparent that the warring parties couldn't solve the problem themselves, they made a direct appeal to the emperor, asking the state to help them resolve an internal church dispute.

It was a seminal moment—a radical departure from the way Christians had previously handled their internal disputes. Centuries earlier, the Apostle Paul wrote to the Corinthian Christians, warning them not to drag their disagreements into court. "Dare any of you," he wrote, "having a matter against another, go to law before the unrighteous and not before the saints? Do you not know that the saints will judge the world? And if the world will be judged by you, are you unworthy to judge the smallest matters?" (1 Corinthians 6:1, 2)

Paul was clear: Christians served a King whose Kingdom was not of this world. For this reason, then, worldly courts had no place arbitrating the internal disputes of the church. However—and this is important to notice—Paul's words show that Christians *do* argue. They are sinners with fallen natures, and the Bible clearly anticipated disputes among believers. The place for mediation, however, is the church, not the courthouse.

Under Constantine, the biblical model changed drastically. The Donatists, no longer fearing any kind of persecution at the hands of the Romans, thought it would be a good idea to let the state decide their case. They appealed to Constantine, who asked the Bishop of Rome to preside over a panel that would, one way or another, make a decision. Should *traditores* be readmitted to the church? Should they be allowed to hold office and perform the rites and rituals of Christianity?

The panel met in October of AD 313 at the Lateran Palace—and ruled against the Donatists. Furious, the Donatists appealed the case, saying that their side had not been given a full hearing. They complained that the Bishop of Rome had stacked the meeting against them, so that they were sure to lose. A frustrated Constantine ordered another meeting, this time in the city of Arles (Arelate), where Constantine's father had established his home after being promoted to Caesar. The meeting took place in AD 314, and this time, Constantine called bishops from all over the empire to convene and decide the matter.

The Donatists fared no better; the second convention also ruled against them. Again, they were furious, and the danger of a serious split remained. It was becoming painfully obvious to Emperor Constantine that the glue for his new empire, the Christian church, might not be as strong as he thought.

At one point, greatly irritated with the feuding Christians, he penned these words:

> So great a madness persists in [the Donatists] that with incredible arrogance they repudiate the equitable judgment that has been given, so that, by the will of heaven, I have learnt that they demand my own judgment. They demand my judgment when I myself await the judgment of Christ.[33]

Constantine believed that if he could not bring unity to the Christian church, God would stop favoring him, and he would never be able unite the Roman Empire. Angry, he told the African church that if they didn't get their act together, he was going to come down *in person* and show them how to run a church. If anyone objected, then, well, to quote Constantine himself: "These without doubt I shall cause to suffer the due penalties of their madness and their reckless obstinacy."[34]

By threatening the use of government force to settle the church controversy, Constantine began mixing church and state in a way that had never happened in the first 300 years of Christianity. He blended the interests of the empire with the life of the church. He even threatened the death penalty for people who didn't toe the line. Some historical records indicate that Caecilian, the bishop who won the Donatist dispute, actually rounded up his opponents with the help of the Roman authorities, and had them put to death.[35]

The blend of church and state was a new paradigm that would last for centuries. It became further entrenched in the next dispute to erupt in the brave new world of state-sponsored Christianity. A priest by the name of Arius, also in North Africa, began to question the full divinity of Christ.

This created a massive uproar within the church, but one of a different nature than the Donatist Controversy. This time it wasn't a matter of church politics—it was purely a doctrinal, theological issue. It touched on a key teaching of the Christian faith: the nature of Jesus, the God-man, the second Person of the Godhead.

Arius had declared that God the Father was too pure and elevated to appear on the earth; therefore, He created the Son, who then created the world. The Son was not equal to the Father, neither was He co-eternal with the Father. Jesus, he said, had a beginning and had "proceeded" from the Father. Of course, He was still elevated far above the rest of creation, and there was no question that He was the Son of God. But He was not fully God, having been created.

His ideas were not original; they could be traced back directly to Paul [the Bishop] of Samosata, who had said similar things more than 50 years earlier. Arius, however, pushed the concept into the limelight.

Of course, if Jesus were not fully God, equal to the Father, then He could not be the same God of redemption found in the Old Testament, and worshipping Him would be tantamount to idolatry.

Eventually, the debate came to focus on two Greek words: *homoousios* and *homoiousios*. To the English mind, the words appear to be separated by the insertion of a single "i", but the actual difference in meaning is far more substantial. *Homoousios* means "of the same substance," that is, Jesus is consubstantial, made of the same substance as the Father. He is equal. *Homoiousios,* with the additional "i", means "of a similar substance," which means that Jesus is *like* the Father, but not really the same.

What Arius proposed was a huge theological no-no, and ran contrary to the opening words of John's gospel. He was fine with Jesus as the Creator of the world, which was explicitly clear in Scripture, but John's description of creation disallowed the notion that Jesus Himself had been created:

> *In the beginning was the Word, and the Word was with God,*
> *and the Word was God. He was in the beginning with God.*
> *All things were made through Him, and without Him noth-*
> *ing was made that was made. (John 1:1-3)*

Notice: *all* things were made by Jesus, and without Him, nothing that was made—nothing that once didn't exist but then came into existence—came into existence without Him. If Jesus had once not existed, then He was also "made," and it was obvious that He could not have made Himself. What Arius was teaching was unscriptural.

Consider, too, the words of Paul in his letter to the Philippians:

> *Therefore God also has highly exalted Him and given Him the name which is above every name, that at the name of Jesus every knee should bow, of those in heaven, and of those on earth, and of those under the earth, and that every tongue should confess that Jesus Christ is Lord, to the glory of God the Father. (Philippians 2:9-11)*

At first glance, there is nothing in the text to suggest that Jesus is equal to the Father, until you consider that Paul is quoting from the Old Testament:

> *Look to Me, and be saved, all you ends of the earth! For I am God, and there is no other. I have sworn by Myself; the word has gone out of My mouth in righteousness, and shall not return, that to Me every knee shall bow, every tongue shall take an oath. (Isaiah 45:22, 23)*

When Paul used this passage from Isaiah to describe the exaltation of Jesus, his original 1st century audience would have immediately picked up on what he was saying: Jesus *is* the God of the Old Testament.

In the same passage, Paul informs the Philippians that Jesus "did not consider it robbery to be equal with God, but made Himself of no reputation." (Philippians 2:6, 7)

If the Christian church as a whole followed Arius' lead and rejected the full divinity of Christ, then it would have profound implications for the doctrine of salvation: it would have meant that someone other than the Old Testament God of salvation had died on the cross, and the worship of Jesus as a mere created being would be inappropriate.

In the early church councils that met in North Africa to deal with Arius' heretical teachings, a bishop asked him if Jesus was *changeable*. If He is created, the bishop asserted, then like all other created beings, He must be subject to change. Arius agreed. After all, Jesus had once not existed and now did, a rather substantive change. The bishop pushed the issue further: if Jesus were subject to change, would it be possible for the Son of God to change from good to evil, the way that Lucifer had? Again, Arius agreed—which, of course, infuriated the assembly.

At first, Constantine failed to grasp the theological gravity of the debate, and dismissed it as a trifling dispute over minor matters. He *was* worried about church disunity, continuing to believe that a disunited church would lead to a disunited empire and that, if the church split, God would refuse to bless his reign. He fired off a letter to the bishops involved, castigating them for splitting the church over matters that were "trifling and of little moment."

While never fully grasping the finer points of theology, Constantine gradually became aware that the dispute was far more substantive than he had at first suspected. He called a meeting in the ancient city of Antioch, one of the key centers of Christianity. After having been pulled into the disputes of the Christian community previously, he now considered himself the de facto head of the Christian church. Even though he had still not been baptized, he was clearly running the show.

He sent his mother's pastor to mediate the discussion.

The Antioch meeting was a failure; it resolved nothing. With the issue festering like an open and deep sore on the church, and with the threat of a split becoming more real, Constantine called another meeting, which became one of the most famous church councils in Christian history. It convened in AD 325 in the present-day city of İznik, Turkey—a city that used to be known as Nicaea.

Today, little is left of the ancient city except for the crumbling ruins of a city wall and a handful of ancient buildings, including a church from Constantine's era that has since been converted into a mosque. There is almost nothing to indicate that one of the most important theological showdowns in Christian history took place there.

Delegates came from all over the empire, and some historical accounts claim that every one them bore the scars of Diocletian's persecution: some were blinded, some were missing limbs, some were covered with burns. Those who led the church in Constantine's time were serious about their faith; a split in the church *had* to be avoided.

At the end of the council, the delegates confirmed what Christians had always believed: Jesus was fully God, co-eternal with the Father. They affirmed *homoousios,* that Jesus was of the same substance as the Father, and they developed the Nicene Creed, a statement of belief that applied to all Christians:

I believe in one God, the Father Almighty, Maker of heaven and earth, and of all things visible and invisible.

And in one Lord Jesus Christ, the only-begotten Son of God, begotten of the Father before all worlds; God of God, Light of Light, very God of very God; begotten, not made, being of one substance with the Father, by whom all things were made.

Who, for us men for our salvation, came down from heaven, and was incarnate by the Holy Spirit of the virgin Mary, and was made man; and was crucified also for us under Pontius Pilate; He suffered and was buried; and the third day He rose again, according to the Scriptures; and ascended into heaven, and sits on the right hand of the Father; and He shall come again, with glory, to judge the quick and the dead; whose kingdom shall have no end.

And I believe in the Holy Ghost, the Lord and Giver of Life; who proceeds from the Father and the Son; who with the Father and the Son together is worshipped and glorified; who spoke by the prophets.

And I believe one holy catholic and apostolic Church. I acknowledge one baptism for the remission of sins; and I look for the resurrection of the dead, and the life of the world to come. Amen.

The creed was developed in Nicaea, underwent some minor revisions at the Council of Constantinople in AD 381, and was confirmed again at the Council of Chalcedon in 451. Christians of various denominational backgrounds have been reciting it ever since.

Arianism was the key subject at the Council of Nicaea; however, knowing that the church had brought the Roman state into its discussions, and that Constantine had become the de facto head of the church, some people have begun to tell a different story about what actually happened in Nicaea.

Some people, for example, have suggested that Constantine essentially invented the divinity of Christ, and led the council to adopt what he personally believed. Prior to his interference, it is said, the church did not accept the full divinity of Jesus.

It doesn't make historical sense, however. Constantine knew little of the debate over Christ's divinity and became involved only when the issue threatened to rip apart the church. Arius was an outlier, someone who had agitated the church with his mostly novel ideas about the nature of Christ. The reason the council was convened was because *most of the church had a problem with Arius.* If the doctrine of Christ's divinity had been inserted into Christianity by Constantine, then why did so many bishops reject Arius' less-than-divine Jesus?

If the divinity of Jesus was essentially a new doctrine to the church in AD 325, it raises another important question: what were the pagan Roman philosophers protesting before that time? One of their primary objections to the faith was the idea that Christians were worshipping a human being as God. Remember: in AD 170, 150 years before Nicaea, the Roman critic Celsus mocked the Christian teaching of the incarnation, saying that a perfect God would never stoop to become a mere human being.

Christians weren't the ones who questioned the divinity of Christ—the pagan Romans did. The Council of Nicaea affirmed Jesus' divinity, but it did not invent it—and neither did Constantine.

The other thing some people say happened in Nicaea is that the council essentially invented the New Testament. It is argued that, before AD 325, there were hundreds of books considered sacred to Christians, as well as dozens of gospels—accounts of the life of Jesus. It is suggested that, at Nicaea, Constantine allowed only the books and gospels that agreed with his own ideas, and rejected the books that didn't teach the divinity of Christ.

Judging from the content of Constantine's letters to the bishops, however, he was a theological lightweight, and he didn't bring much in the way of personal theology to the debate because he didn't have much. From the moment he became aware of the dispute, he was continually playing catch-up. To suggest that his own theology drove the debate is nonsense.

We also know that the canon of the New Testament was well-established before the council met. The early church fathers made clear reference to the books we still have in the New Testament. In AD 180, for example, Ireneaus of Lyons referred to four gospels:

> It is not possible that the Gospels can be either more or fewer in number than they are. For, since there are four zones of the world in which we live, and four principal winds, while the Church is scattered throughout all the world, and the "pillar and ground" of the Church is the Gospel and the spirit of life; it is fitting that she should have four pillars, breathing out immortality on every side, and vivifying men afresh. From which fact, it is evident that the Word, the Artificer of all, He that sitteth upon the cherubim, and contains all things, He who was manifested to men, has given us the Gospel under four aspects, but bound together by one Spirit.[36]

If the Christians had dozens of gospels before the Council of Nicaea, it leaves one to wonder how Ireneaus could be so certain that the number of established gospels—four—was the ideal number, and God's perfect design?

The canon of the New Testament was well defined by the time the Council of Nicaea met, and the divinity of Christ was well understood by the time Jesus returned to heaven. As much as skeptics might want the Christian church to be an invention of Constantine, it's just not true.

That doesn't mean, however, that Constantine didn't change *something*. He did, and it was not a healthy development for the church. The Council of Nicaea underscored his new role as the head of the Christian church, and helped seal the marriage of church and state that would define the church from that day forward. Prior to Constantine, the state persecuted Christians and tried to sway them away from their monotheistic beliefs, but it did not play a role in defining the church itself. In a radical departure from the New Testament model of church governance, the state started deciding cases for the church.

In Nicaea, fortunately, the council arrived at the right decision—but they had the wrong person presiding over the debate. It should not have been the Roman emperor, especially one whose own Christianity was unclear. The standard of truth for Christians is not the state, not the emperor, but the Scriptures. "All Scripture is given by inspiration of God," Paul wrote to Timothy, "and is profitable for doctrine, for reproof, for correction, for instruction in righteousness, that the man of God may be complete, thoroughly equipped for every good work." (2 Timothy 3:16, 17)

The Christians didn't really need the emperor. They had everything they needed to run the church and make decisions about faith, because they had the Bible. Jesus was crystal clear: "My kingdom is not of this world." (John 18:36)

Starting in the 4th century, however, when the favor of the emperor fell on the church, and the ranks of believers were flooded with opportunity-seekers from the general Roman public, our Christian ancestors launched something of a shadow empire. It looked like Christianity, and it sounded like Christianity, but it had some real problems. The life of the church was now intimately entwined with the Roman Empire. Roman-style politics found their way into church governance. Over the years, as Christianity lurched toward the Dark Ages, the church became less about fulfilling the Gospel Commission and anticipating the long-awaited Kingdom of Christ, and more about the governments of Rome's European successors.

With the Roman emperor at the head of the church, we began to feel free to handle matters the same way that Constantine did: we used coercion rather than persuasion. After the Donatist Controversy was settled, for example, historical records indicate that Caecilian, the Bishop of Carthage, rounded up a number of Donatus' followers with the assistance of the Roman authorities and had them put to death.

After Constantine, many Christians stopped living by the words of Jesus: "Render therefore to Caesar the things that are Caesar's, and to God the things that are God's." Instead, we started blending the things of God with the things of Caesar, and history has shown that this it not a healthy move for the church. The state tragically started using force to run the church, to the point where Constantine even passed one of the very first blue laws, a law forbidding work on Sunday:

> On the venerable Day of the Sun let the magistrates and people residing in cities rest, and let all workshops be closed.

In the country, however, persons engaged in agriculture may freely and lawfully continue their pursuits; because it often happens that another day is not so suitable for grain-sowing or for vine-planting; lest by neglecting the proper moment for such operations the bounty of heaven should be lost.[37]

In AD 321, of course, Constantine had not been baptized or openly declared his Christianity. He was profoundly influenced by Christianity, but had not entirely forsaken paganism, which is likely why he referred to the first day of the week as the "venerable Day of the Sun." The "sun day" was an important festival to the pagan Romans, and Constantine "christianized" it, using the force of government to make it mandatory.

Constantine's marriage of church and state continued well into the history of medieval Europe. He created an environment where, eventually, it wasn't just the state running the church, but it was also the church running the state. The adoption of Roman coercion led directly to the heretic trials, torture chambers, and horrific executions carried out under the banner of Christ and mocked by skeptics of Christianity to this day. It was no longer Romans persecuting Christians, but Christians persecuting each other. Once the victims of religious oppression, we refused to grant religious liberty to each other.

Once we blurred the lines between Caesar and Christ, between church and state, Christians became a tool of the state, and vice-versa. The Roman basilica became the Christian basilica, and eventually, when the Roman emperors all moved east to Constantinople, the Christian church actually became the de facto Caesar in the west.

But did Jesus, even for a moment, ever employ the power of the state to force belief in Himself? On the contrary—He was executed by the state!

Today, much of the world looks on Christians with a great deal of skepticism, and if Christians were honest with history, they would have to admit that to some extent, they've earned it. Giddy with the sudden relief and liberty granted by the enthronement of Constantine and the Edict of Milan, we allowed a tectonic shift in the structure of the Christian church. We began to live in the empire of Constantine rather than the empire of Christ. Instead of anticipating the coming Kingdom that Jesus promised to establish when He returned, we forgot Daniel's assertion that God's Kingdom would be inaugurated "without hands." We began to build a temporal empire, assuming that God wanted *us* to build it *with* hands.

The Bible, however, teaches that human empires stand in the way of Christ's Kingdom and will be swept away.

Today, many Christians enjoy unprecedented liberty, living in perhaps the freest society in the history of the planet. American Christians in particular enjoy an entrenched separation of church and state, where the government is not permitted to seize the reins of the church, and sectarian groups cannot seize the reins of government. At the moment, we are certainly freer than the Christians who were forced to endure a new kind of persecution throughout the Dark Ages, living in fear that they might be accused of disagreeing with official doctrine.

We must not take our liberty for granted.

In the 1980s, however, in the face of rapid moral decay in the West, many Christians started to question the idea of separating the church from the state. We started to suggest that perhaps some atheist—maybe even the Soviets—invented the idea of the separation of church and state as a way to undermine the Christian religion. In a sad twist of fate, some Christians started to suggest that the separation of church and state is actually a hindrance to the Christian faith, because it prevents the establishment of a truly Christian nation.

Living under the shadow of Constantine, some people have begun to suggest that the best way for Christians to secure their future is to win at the ballot box, to seize the reins of government and once again make Christianity the official state religion. Some people appear to be longing for the mechanisms of the state to not only *permit* their religion, but to endorse and promote it.

During the late 1980s and through the 1990s, American politics was permeated by calls for Christians—through movements such as (but not limited to) the Christian Coalition—to take control of the White House and Congress. Such movements adopted an almost millennialist flavor, apparently working under the assumption that God wanted *through the power of human government* for Christians to usher in the Kingdom of God on Earth.

Should Christians vote their conscience? Yes. Should Christians be active in civil matters? Of course. Are Christians a key part of the American fabric (or the fabric of many other nations?) Naturally. Christians have as much right to live peaceably in a nation as does anybody else. Their natural rights are the same as everyone else's.

But should Christians use the state to coerce non-Christians to support and/or endorse their beliefs and lifestyle?

That is not so clear.

At the time of this writing, there have been a number of highly publicized examples of Christians who blurred the line between proselytizing (appropriate for any religion) and coercion (inappropriate for the religion of Christ). One notable example is that of former pastor Joshua Feuerstein, who in 2015, decried a supposed lack of Christmas symbolism on Starbucks' coffee cups.

For Christians, it is easy to sympathize with Feuerstein's dismay that Christians and Christianity appear to be falling out of favor with Western culture. Many people are naturally perturbed by what appears to be an effort to eliminate Christian religious symbols and festivals from the public eye. School Christmas programs have been dropped in many places and replaced with winter festivals, so as not to "offend" non-Christians. There are court challenges to nativity scenes erected on public land.

Some Christians feel as if their religion is no longer wanted, while they perceive non-Christian faiths as receiving special accommodation. Thus, it is easy to see why some Christians feel marginalized.

Enter Feuerstein, who became bothered when he found little evidence of Christmas on Starbucks' 2015 seasonal coffee cups. The cups were plain, red in color and featured only the iconic Starbucks logo. It didn't seem to matter that Starbucks features many Christmas products—clearly marked as such. What mattered to him, apparently, was that the cups were plain, and that the baristas were not required to wish him a merry Christmas.

To force the issue, Feuerstein gave his name to the barista as "Merry Christmas." That way, when his order was ready, the staff would have to call him by the Christmas greeting. He triumphantly went online to tell the world how he'd pulled a fast one on Starbucks, and called for Christians to boycott the corporation for not supporting Christmas.

Many Christians applauded, feeling some vindication. But what they quickly forgot was the chagrin they felt when Christian bakery owners were required by law to provide wedding cakes for same-sex marriages. They rightly felt that nobody should be coerced into participating in events that violated their own conscience.

To be sure, Feuerstein did not appeal to the state in order to force the issue; there is no law requiring corporations to decorate for Christmas. But he did resort to coercion, a Christian weakness that hails back to the days when Constantine put the power of the state at the disposal of the Christian church.

We quickly forget that such coercive tactics were once used against us. We would like to be free to worship God according to the dictates of conscience. In order to be free, we must understand that the same liberty must be granted to all. If Starbucks wanted to celebrate Ramadan instead of Christmas, that is their right. And if Christians want a distinctly Christian restaurant, it is their right to open one.

Feuerstein's social media campaign was not a matter of church and state; it was simply a matter of coercion. Shortly after the Starbucks brouhaha, a case erupted in Great Britain, where the Church of England wanted to air a pro-prayer advertisement in theaters that coincided with the much-hyped *Star Wars: The Force Awakens* release in December of 2015.

The commercial was well-produced and emotionally appealing. It was simply a recitation of the Lord's Prayer, one phrase at a time, by people from virtually all walks of life. It ended with an appeal to visit a website dedicated to the subject of prayer. There was no finger-pointing, there was no defamation of other faith groups—it was simply the words to the Lord's Prayer.

Digital Cinema Media (the corporation responsible for placing in-theater advertising), however, deemed the commercial as too potentially offensive to air in theaters. They were apparently afraid of a backlash from non-Christian audience members, and the ad was rejected.

It is questionable that any significant backlash would have materialized, and Christians were naturally saddened by the news that the mere words of Jesus would be deemed inappropriate for public consumption. The average movie trailer, saturated with edgy sexuality, graphic violence, and over-spiritualism, has far more potential to offend, to which any parent who suddenly had to distract a child from on-screen content can testify.

Those who were offended by DCM's decision, as of the time of this writing, were preparing to mount a lawsuit. Given the highly litigious nature of modern Western civilization, such a response was hardly surprising. It's what we do: when offended, we sue.

Before using the state to force others to provide a platform for the Gospel, however, Christians ought to carefully consider whether state coercion is the *biblical* response. Nobody likes to be discriminated against. In that, modern Christians are like any other group that has been marginalized or excluded from the arena of public thought.

But is state coercion the way Jesus would solve the problem? What part of the Gospel Commission—the God-given assignment of the church—would a public lawsuit achieve?

It is important for Christians to remember that, by and large, corporations who do not wish to do business with us are not our property. Private companies do not *owe* us advertising contracts. If it were a matter of *breach* of contract—a company going back on the terms of a signed contract—that might be a different story. Like any other citizen, we would have the right to hold them to the legal terms of the agreement.

But we cannot *force* people to do business with us, or to do our business *for* us. Hard feelings are understandable; nobody likes to be rejected. There is little question that DCM's decision was prejudicial, but Christians cannot afford to compromise the Gospel by forcing people to publish our views. Check the New Testament carefully; Jesus never instructed His disciples to force the state to champion His cause.

It is not up to others to share the Gospel; it is the responsibility of Christians—by whatever means necessary, with one notable exception: coercion. Coercion does not accomplish the work of Christ.

Look back over the long and shameful legacy of medieval Christianity. It becomes obvious that coercion has done far more harm than good. We forced Jews to convert or lose their property, forcing thousands to leave Western Europe in search of new homes. We put heretics on trial, and used the power of the state to torture and execute them. And nowhere did the Scriptures endorse such things.

"My kingdom," Jesus said, facing Pontius Pilate, "is not of this world. If My kingdom were of this world, My servants would fight, so that I should not be delivered to the Jews; but now My kingdom is not from here." (John 18:36)

It would be *unnatural* for a Christian not to be keenly disappointed by an advertising company's decision to exclude them. That is understandable. A personal appeal to the corporation would also be understandable—and appropriate. But a lawsuit?

Imagine an atheist group insisting that a privately-owned Christian television station be forced to air *their* content. It is almost always a useful exercise, when considering matters of religious liberty, to turn the tables and apply the Golden Rule. Would I want someone else to force *me* to do the same thing?

The reality is that Christianity has seldom enjoyed the applause of popular culture. In fact, with the exception of a handful of short historical periods, it has almost *never* enjoyed it. If Christians wish to air ads in theaters, and the theaters don't want it, there are a couple appropriate responses. You could (a) purchase a theater and run the ads to your heart's content, or (b) follow the advice of Jesus: wipe the dust off your feet and move on:

> *And whoever will not receive you, when you go out of that city, shake off the very dust from your feet as a testimony against them. (Luke 9:5)*

In other words, leave it to God to deal with those who reject Him. Remember, it was not a member of the church who convinced Saul of Tarsus to stop persecuting Christians; it was Christ Himself. And even Jesus, when faced with those who rejected His message, allowed them to simply walk away (see John 6:66). You'll never find Him running to the Romans, looking for state support to coerce a hearing.

There *is* a fight in which Christians should engage: the fight for liberty—both for themselves and for others. If we long to be free to preach the Gospel, we ought to be the first to support the rest of the world's right to speak its mind as well.

Using the power of the state to promote our faith? It's an uneasy partnership that always ends badly. We must never forget that it has been tried, and it led Christians to behave more like Diocletian than like Jesus of Nazareth. We built a shadow empire, a Christianity reared in the image of the Romans. It *looked* like Christianity, with much of the same language and religious trappings, but it essentially recreated Jesus in the image of the Caesar. There is much blood on Christian hands, and what happened is impossible to reconcile with the teachings of the humble Carpenter from Nazareth.

You and I have an important decision to make: do we serve Caesar or Jesus? It doesn't mean that Christians do not participate in civil life, or even that they do not run for office. While Christians are not ultimately *of* the world, we are still in it, and the Bible instructs us to live peaceably with the community, obey the powers that be, and live as good citizens to the extent that civil powers do not require us to forsake Christ.

But as we participate in the world around us, we must never forget who our ultimate King is. If there is a discrepancy between what Caesar requires and what Jesus desires, there is no choice for the Christian but to cast his or her lot with the King of kings.

We cannot allow ourselves to repeat past mistakes. For the time being, the shadows cast over Christianity by the empire of Constantine have been pushed back, at least in the West. We cannot forget, however, that there have always been, and always will be, forces that long to coerce. The story is not finished. Just as the book of Revelation so accurately predicted the Diocletian persecution, it also predicts a return to religious persecution:

> He was granted power to give breath to the image of the beast, that the image of the beast should both speak and cause as many as would not worship the image of the beast to be killed. (Revelation 13:15)

There is a moment coming when, again, the power of the state will be wielded against those whose highest allegiance is to Jesus. The Christian church has already passed through two such phases. First, we suffered through the religious persecution of pagan Roman emperors. Second, after Constantine, when the power of Caesar was granted to the church, we used the power of the state against each other.

We cannot do it again. When coercive religion comes—and according to John, it will—we must recognize it and reject it. The shadow of Constantine, the child born of a one-night stand, still lurks in the fallen hearts of men. It will be there until God abolishes human empires and establishes His own:

> *And in the days of these kings the God of heaven will set up a kingdom which shall never be destroyed; and the kingdom shall not be left to other people; it shall break in pieces and consume all these kingdoms, and it shall stand forever. (Daniel 2:44)*

FOOTNOTES FOR CHAPTER FIVE

31. Kousoulas, D. George. *The Life and Times of Constantine the Great.* Bethesda, MD: Rutledge, 2007. Print, 380.

32. *Translations and Reprints from the Original Sources of European History, Vol. 4,* 1st Ed. Philadelphia: U of Pennsylvania, 1897. Print, 28-30.

33. Stephenson, Paul. *Constantine: Roman Emperor, Christian Victor.* New York: Overlook, 2010. Print, 262.

34. Ibid., 263.

35. Ibid., 264.

36. Irenaeus. *Against Heresies.* Print.

37. Schaff, Philip. *History of the Christian Church, Vol. 3,* 5th Ed. New York: C. Scribner's Sons, 1902. Print, 380.